D1565012

eSports is Business

Tobias M. Scholz

eSports is Business

Management in the World of Competitive Gaming

Tobias M. Scholz
University of Siegen
Siegen, Germany

ISBN 978-3-030-11198-4   ISBN 978-3-030-11199-1   (eBook)
https://doi.org/10.1007/978-3-030-11199-1

Library of Congress Control Number: 2019931908

This Palgrave Pivot imprint is published by the registered company Springer Nature Switzerland AG
The registered company address is: Gewerbestrasse 11, 6330 Cham, Switzerland

Preface

The one thing you should know about eSports is that it is moving fast, and it has been doing that for decades. In my early days in eSports (around 2003 and 2004), I was the editor-in-chief for a German magazine dedicated solely to eSports. Already back then, the questions were which tournaments you cover, which events are relevant, and what can you cover within the limited space of a magazine. In the preparation for this book, I read old issues of that magazine and looked into the documents I had hoarded from that time. Back then, eSports was emerging: it was quite painful to watch the tournaments, but it was already a big thing, in its niche. There were discussions about being part of the Olympics, driven by already existing eSports federations, and non-endemic sponsors like Subway were involved in eSports. There were stars, and we experienced a highly fragmented market. Maybe some of you remember the *Enemy Territory* tournaments? It becomes evident that eSports is an umbrella term for competitive gaming and a whole industry comprising various actors. That was the same then; and, based on that history, there are observable patterns that describe the industry and the world of eSports today. This is the goal of this book—to give insights into this unique and different industry and supply you, the reader, with an in-depth understanding of it.

There is an emerging community of eSports researchers, and all of them are doing essential work that inspired my research. Beyond that, the following researchers and eSports individuals helped me move toward a more holistic observation of eSports: Chris Flato, Chris Hana, Julia and David Hiltscher, Jong Seong Kim, Henry Lowood, Florian Neus, Frederic Nimmermann, Will Partin, Robin Reitz, Christian Scholz, Volker Stein, TL Taylor, Steve Wildman, and Emma Witkowski. Furthermore, I want to thank Maria Scholz and Lisa Völkel for their support in the research process. And, finally, I want to thank our university team of the Siegen Bisons, who constantly show me why eSports is such a fascinating and exciting environment to research and to be a part of.

Although certain governing principles and patterns are observable and, at the meta-level, many aspects are explainable, eSports is still highly volatile and fast-paced. I experienced that first hand (again) when I was writing this book: every day something new happened and exciting stories emerged—for example, the franchising of the European League of Legends scene. Furthermore, there are signs that the eSports industry is potentially overheating. We may be in another bubble at the moment and in line for a downfall over the coming months or years. Many actors outside the eSports industry are throwing money at it because of a fear of missing out. The good news is that eSports has been there before, and it helped to grow the business of eSports substantially. Especially in an emerging industry, having a healthy business model is essential, but it is unclear what a robust business model will look like. This book will contribute to the research on eSports management and how to do business in eSports. It becomes clear, then, that eSports will grow, but not all businesses will participate in this growth and will survive.

Good luck and have fun.

Siegen, Germany   Tobias M. Scholz
November 2018

Contents

Abbreviations

AMD	Advanced Micro Devices
BIG	Berlin International Gaming
CBS	Columbia Broadcasting System
CGS	Championship Gaming Series
CPL	Cyberathlete Professional League
CS:GO	Counter-Strike: Global Offensive
CSPPA	Counter-Strike Professional Players' Association
CXG	Cyber X Games
DeCL	Deutschen Clanliga
DeSpV	Deutsche eSport Verband
DeSV	Deutsche eSport Verband e.V.
DotA	Defense of the Ancients
ESB	Deutsche eSport-Bund
ESBD	eSport-Bund Deutschland
ESC	Esports Charts
ESIC	Esports Integrity Coalition
ESL	Electronic Sports League
ESPN	Entertainment and Sports Programming Network
ESWC	Electronic Sports World Cup
FIFA	Fédération Internationale de Football Association
HLTV	Half-Life Television
IeSf	International e-Sports Federation
IOC	International Olympic Committee

IPTV	Internet Protocol Television
KeSPA	Korean e-Sports Association
LAN	Local Area Network
LCS	League of Legends Championship Series
LoL	League of Legends
MLG	Major League Gaming
MOBA	Multiplayer Online Battle Arena
Mod	Modification
MTG	Modern Times Group
MTV	Music Television
Na'Vi	Natus Vincere
NBA	National Basketball Association
NBC	National Broadcasting Company
NCAA	National Collegiate Athletic Association
NFL	National Football League
NiP	Ninjas in Pyjamas
OGN	OnGameNet
OWL	Overwatch League
PGL	Professional Gamers League
PSG	Paris Saint-Germain Football Club
PUBG	PlayerUnknown's Battlegrounds
PvE	Player versus Environment
PvP	Player versus Player
TBS	Turner Broadcasting System
Team WE	Team World Elite
WADA	World Anti-Doping Agency
WCG	World Cyber Games
WESA	World Esports Association
WSVG	World Series of Video Games

List of Figures

List of Tables

1

Introduction: The Emergence of eSports

Abstract The world of eSports or competitive gaming has grown exponentially in recent years; however, the industry itself is not as young as
many believe. There are many similarities with traditional sports and
media businesses, but there are many differences, too, in the eSports
industry. With the absence of a standardized governance structure,
eSports is predominantly self-organizing and mostly business-driven.
Primarily due to the young audience, the global approach, and the digitized environment, the eSports industry does not follow traditional business rules. Consequently, an observation of the history from a business
perspective and an in-depth analysis of the strategic management are necessary to categorize the eSports industry.

Keywords eSports • Competitive gaming • Business model • Strategic
management

T. M. Scholz, *eSports is Business*, https://doi.org/10.1007/978-3-030-11199-1_1

1

The Relevance of eSports for Today's Businesses

For the citizens of Katowice in Poland, it is nowadays a familiar sight: tens of thousands of young people visit their city to watch people play video games. It may still seem strange for some inhabitants, but what they experience are enthusiastic fans extensively cheering for their respective teams. It was a bit of luck that the tournament organizer ESL chose Katowice in 2013 as one of the leading managers has his roots in Katowice, but the tournament became the most entertaining event in eSports quickly. The polish crowd and many international visitors show every year how great eSports tournaments can be. The competition in Katowice is a prime example of how far eSports came in its short history. If people ask me what makes eSports great, those tournaments are the best example for it—a global and digital phenomenon that lures people away from their digital devices actually to go into an arena and celebrate with other eSports-nerds.

The term 'eSports' is a portmanteau of 'electronic' and 'sports' and is sometimes described as competitive gaming. The idea of playing games is profoundly entangled with human society: indeed, Huizinga (1949) considers play to be an existential part of humanity, describing it as *Homo Ludens*. Technological development allowed this ludic drive to expand into the digital world, creating video games. It is important to highlight that the first games were already focusing on the competitive aspect and, more importantly, creating an environment in which people could watch the competitors play. The first game for entertainment purposes was the *Tennis for Two* by William Higinbotham in 1958: this already had a competitive aspect as well as the inherent potential to let others watch the game (Wolf 2012).

After 1958, video games grew exponentially in line with technological progress and gained extreme momentum through developments like the personal computer, the internet, and, today, the smartphone. The market for video games consists of 2 billion people who play at least casually (Skaugen 2015). Furthermore, the aspect of competition, as in traditional sports, is essential for the growth of video games. People want to watch professional players show their skills, and this is one explanation for people watching other people playing video games. For example, over 80 million individual viewers watched the 2017 *League of Legends* World Championship between SK Telecom T1 (South Korea) and Royal Never Give Up (China) (Riot 2017). Although viewership numbers are difficult to measure in both traditional media and online media, and the numbers are often criticized for being inaccurate (Hetsroni and Tukachinsky 2006), they give a hint as to the potential of eSports. Beyond the human motivation to play and watch play, eSports, like any other traditional sport, is big business.

However, eSports is not comparable with sports like American or European football, as eSports is more an umbrella term for any video game that can be played competitively. A prominent definition of eSports was offered by Wagner: "ESports is an area of sport activities in which people develop and train mental or physical abilities in the use of information and communication technologies" (2006, p. 3). Arnaud complements Wagner's definition: "Passion, training, reflex, intelligence and teamwork … if it's not sport it really has its taste" (2010, p. 11). It is observable that eSports is still an emerging market and its potential growth seems limitless. Based on its rate of growth, analysts predict that eSports may become "the next big thing in media and entertainment" (Takahashi 2015), with some concluding that "resistance is futile" (Casselmann 2015). The CEO of Logitech Darrell even predicts that "it'll be the biggest sport in the world" (Darrell 2018). Examples are Amazon's acquisition of the video game live streaming service Twitch for $970 million (Amazon 2014) and the investment of traditional sports teams in eSports. In 2017 and 2018, sports organizations spent $400 million on franchise fees alone (Wolf 2018). Sponsoring ranges from endemic companies like Intel to non-endemics like DHL, Mercedes-Benz, and even Wüstenrot (a German home purchase savings company).

Still, eSports is an emerging and growing market moving toward $1 billion market revenues in 2018 (Newzoo 2018), and the market is observably increasing; however, being part of a growing industry and hoping for a solid return on investment is not the only driver to join the eSports industry. There are five important reasons for people and companies to get involved in eSports.

Firstly, eSports reaches a digital and international audience. Being an industry based on a digital product like video games, it becomes evident that the product and the industry are highly digital. Furthermore, because of the growth of the internet, eSports are highly international, and people from various countries play together. The eSports industry is, therefore, a highly compelling case, as it is born global and born digital, turning analog and local—quite the opposite to every other industry that is generally born local and analog first. Companies, in general, can learn from eSports and try to incorporate these lessons in their digitization and internationalization strategies.

Secondly, the player base and fan base in eSports are exceptionally young compared to other traditional sports. Traditional sports are struggling with the situation that their viewership is going gray. For example, the NFL has an average age of 50 years in its viewership, moving up from 46 in 2006. Even football has an average of 39 years, moving up from 35 years in 2006 (Lombardo and Broughton 2017). Some statistics declare that the average eSports audience is aged from 18 to 34 (Bathurst 2017; Nielsen 2017). Consequently, while organizations—especially sports organizations—struggle to reach a young audience, eSports represents a significant portion of this young audience. Any investment in eSports that turns into a spillover effect, slowing or reversing the going gray effect, will amortize the investment quickly.

Thirdly, in terms of maturity, the industry is still emerging. Structures are still growing and evolving; new companies are entering the market, and both the market entry barriers and the market exit barriers are low. Although this is slowly changing, and we can already observe that companies are being increasingly cautious, it can be stated that a company entering the eSports industry now can be categorized as an early adopter—or, more precisely, a lagging early adopter. However, this may not be the case for every aspect of the industry. For example, sports organizations have moved massively into eSports. At the end of 2017, around 50 sports organizations were investing in eSports; today, there are over 250 sports organizations involved. However, it is still possible to have a top professional eSports team with an investment of $5 million. It is observable, though, that the eSports industry is leaving the early adopter phase, and many companies are stating that they are moving beyond their start-up phase.

Fourthly, an interesting aspect of the eSports industry is a significant difference from traditional sports. Contrary to traditional sports, eSports is industry-driven. It is necessary to clarify that games like American and European football are at the professional level highly industry-driven and even a federation like FIFA follows the market rules, but the sports football is not industry-driven. Sports like football grew over time and were created by a particular group of people playing; therefore, the rules of sports evolved. This is the main difference from eSports, as any eSports title is based on a video game, and such a video game is created, designed, and curated by a video game developer. Consequently, the video game developer is the gatekeeper that watches over the video game. Hence, any video game developer with an eSports title has the power to change the rules, create new content, and ultimately pull the plug. As the video game developer is often a business company, it has to follow the market, but theoretically, Valve Software could shut down its *Counter-Strike* game tomorrow. Federations like FIFA would not be able to stop any football player playing football.

Finally, competitive gaming is now 60 years old, and eSports in its current form is roughly 20 years old: in this time, eSports has been relatively isolated and often branded as a nerd phenomenon (Schutz 2018), and, consequently, ignored by the rest of the world. The eSports industry, except for South Korea, has had time to grow on its own and create its own rules and principles. Furthermore, without an overarching governance structure and outside pressure, the eSports industry has been mostly self-regulated. That has allowed the industry to be innovative and selectively copy structures from other sectors. Nobody has imposed existing structures on the eSports industry, and, most of the time, eSports has had the space to grow on its own.

These factors show the potential interest from companies; still, they do not explain the explosion of eSports in recent years. The critical turning point was a combination of several acquisitions in 2014 and 2015 that marked the start of the current and ongoing wave of organizations investing in eSports. One significant acquisition was that of Twitch by Amazon. Although it is still unclear what exactly Amazon's business plan for Twitch is, it showed the interest of the market, especially as Google and several other companies were also interested (Byford 2014).

Furthermore, the media company Modern Times Group (MTG) acquired ESL and DreamHack (both are popular tournament operators in Europe with a good track record in expanding globally), creating a new global player in the eSports industry. Also, investment groups became active with the founding of the eSports organization NRG eSports and Immortals. Finally, 2015 sparked a new era of sports organizations in eSports. The Beşiktaş e-Sports Club was opened by the Beşiktaş J.K. sports organization, after the shutdown of SSV Lehnitz (2002–2006), the first sports organization actively committing to eSports.

Understanding eSports Is More Than Just Another Hype

These critical developments happening in 2014 and 2015 sparked an economic boost that is ongoing. This economic boost shifted the general perception of eSports from just a fad toward a real, exciting, and emerging business sector. Still, eSports is often described as the Wild West, being largely seen as an unregulated and ungoverned phenomenon. The crucial aspect of eSports in general is that it challenges existing structures and, most importantly, existing business models. Interestingly, eSports in its entirety is not a risky business, and a good manager always finds a profitable space in the industry. Over time, specific self-regulation has been established, and governance structures introduced where necessary or required. The Wild West metaphor derives from the situation that existing business models do not necessarily work and that methods of creating a business plan are complicated. For example, risk evaluation is a crucial part of any business model and depends on market data, experts, and analysts; however, cases like Twitch showed that risk evaluation is not possible because the product is so novel and the market is unknown. There is no existing business model to lean on or to copy. Importantly, while eSports and technology are strongly intertwined, technology has been a driver rather than an obstacle to a successful business model. Digitization is not a challenge or a risk, but an exciting opportunity for eSports. Consequently, due to the uniqueness of the eSports industry and the cutting-edge utilization of digitization, it is understandable that it may look like the Wild West from the outside, but eSports could be compared to the work of pioneers preparing for colonization.

The eSports ecosystem is, therefore, different from the existing business understanding. Primarily due to its time evolving on its own, the eSports ecosystem has created unique business models that only partly follow the market logic established in traditional industries. Furthermore, every other sector may have an interest in investing in eSports, leading to a situation where not only entrepreneurs are keen to participate but also traditional media companies, sports organizations, or any other brand that may be interested in reaching a young audience. Consequently, there is an observable clash of business models, leading to a high degree of dynamism. The eSports ecosystem is facing an externally induced change that could transform it fundamentally. However, it is striking that the traditional industries and their established business models are in the role of challenging the younger and less structured industry. The old world has invaded the new world. How this clash will evolve is currently open and, in this dynamic industry, not predictable.

Although eSports has a strong focus on business, research on the business side of eSports is currently quite scarce. Most of the literature focuses on the social phenomenon and how eSports is connecting people (Taylor 2016): the business side is rarely the focus. There is some literature concerning intercultural management (Stein and Scholz 2016) or marketing (Seo 2016; Seo and Jung 2016), in the context of play as work (Brock 2017), property rights (Comerford 2012; Burk 2013), sports management (Cunningham et al. 2018; Funk et al. 2018), and team coordination (Freeman and Wohn 2018; Scholz and Stein 2017; Parshakov et al. 2018). Still, not much research is being done on the business model, the ecosystem, and the actors in the eSports industry. Furthermore, there is a lack of historical observations concerning the business side of eSports. However, in recent years, an increase in business analysts and consulting agencies is observable. Consequently, metrics and numbers are becoming available and shedding some light on the eSports business.

Framing eSports

As mentioned, the eSports industry is acting without a clear governing body, and in certain aspects, there is some form of self-regulation. However, there are also topics that are highly debated, and no final solution is derived. A good example, and essential to discuss in the introduction, is the way eSports is written. From a cultural perspective, there is a tendency in the Anglo-American area to write 'esports', while in Europe 'eSports' is the dominant form, and Asia often writes 'e-Sports'. Even journalism is split on this topic: the Associated Press states that 'esports' is the right form, *The Guardian* writes 'eSports', and the *New York Times* writes 'e-sports'. The same situation is true for the academic scene. Therefore, I looked at the scholarly articles written since 2016 and looked at the spelling. In 40 papers, the term 'eSports' (singular and plural) was used 23 times. Although the debate is still ongoing and will require a linguistic discourse, the majority use of 'eSports' is why this spelling is used here.

The wording of eSports highlights a different aspect concerning the framing of this industry. In the discourse, eSports is often discussed as being a distinct entity that is a sufficient description of the phenomenon. But eSports is not as precise as some think: it is difficult to understand and, most importantly, not self-explainable. Maybe it could be compared to the other big thing we often discuss nowadays, the Blockchain. Everybody is talking about the Blockchain, but only a few truly understand it; furthermore, even fewer know how to make a profit from the Blockchain.

There are two aspects that frame the eSports industry and all actors involved in eSports. On the one hand, eSports is an umbrella term for any game that can be used in competitive gaming; therefore, 'eSports' is similar to the term 'sports'. Talking about a singular entity will not describe eSports in general. There are certain communities for different games, there are region-specific characteristics, and there are various stakeholders involved. For example, there was a tournament in Genting, Malaysia, because *Dota 2* is extremely popular there, combined with a unique set of sponsors.

On the other hand, the eSports industry is highly volatile, and, especially regarding eSports titles, there is high fluctuation as video games have a finite lifespan. Compared to other traditional sports, this is unrivaled. One of the oldest eSports titles played today is *StarCraft* from 1998. In that time, there have been four different iterations of the game. That is a significant difference, as traditional sports may have experienced a gradual evolution, but the eSports titles continuously shift and revolutionize the eSports industry every three to five years. Therefore, the eSports industry may not entirely follow the traditional rules of management and business endeavors. Applying those rules will lead to different results, and the history of eSports reveals that understanding the eSports principles is essential for the long-term survival of any eSports business.

Structure and Theoretical Foundation of the Book

The focus of this book is on the business side of eSports. Therefore, the theoretical foundation will be rooted in strategic management theory (Drucker 1954), assuming "a Schumpeterian world of innovation-based competition, price/performance rivalry, increasing returns, and the 'creative destruction' of existing competences" (Teece et al. 1997, p. 509). The focus of strategic management lies in the evaluation and analysis of the environment as well as the potential for an organization to establish an appropriate strategy that utilizes its potential competitive advantage. "Strategy is the determination of the basic long-term goals of an enterprise, and the adoption of courses of action and the allocation of resources necessary for carrying out these goals" (Chandler 1962, p. 13). Therefore, it is essential to understand what the eSports ecosystem looks like, which stakeholders are involved, and how the business models in eSports can be described. Organizations that are able to utilize their capabilities in this area by adapting, reconfiguring, or diverging from their environment can increase their survivability. However, many aspects influence the current stage of the eSports industry, be it cultural differences, the financial crisis, technological advancements, or the dynamism or uncontrollability of the eSports scene. The eSports industry may seem diverse from the outside, but keep in mind that eSports consist of various disciplines, many different actors, and an ever-increasing number of new actors on the scene.

Furthermore, from an academic perspective, the most striking aspect of eSports is that its strategic management differs from the traditional understanding. Especially concerning business models, in general it is possible to analyze the market, evaluate the risks, and, subsequently, make the growth of an organization manageable. In eSports, however, there is still a lack of data and numbers; there is no common understanding about indicators, creating a business model without numbers, without having an in-depth knowledge, and without the ability to evaluate the risk of a new eSports business endeavor. For example, Twitch took a leap of faith with online streaming without knowing at all if this business model could be profitable. Still, strategic management in eSports is not riskier or less long-term: many organizations know that they have blind spots and that there is a high risk in their business model. That knowledge, at least for the professional eSports organizations, makes the difference and heightens the sensitivity for the market of such organizations. They naturally deal and work with uncertainty, a survival trait for a future in business. For many traditional organizations, the risk of the business model is often shifted by more data and more analysis. The price, however, is the innovativeness of those organizations, as they become predictable. In these modern and volatile times, a predictable organization will become replaceable, as it will lag behind any new technologies and trends, only reacting. The approach of dealing with blind spots and potential risks in the business model is something many organizations could learn from. It may be especially interesting for organizations joining the eSports sector to understand this environment extensively so the organizations can achieve a strategic fit (Scholz 1987) to improve their success in this industry.

An interesting development can be observed in recent years. The eSports industry is categorized as being entirely digital, global, and agile; consequently, eSports organizations seem like the typical organization that is popular in modern management literature. They are capable of combining the challenge of digitization, globalization, and agility; many traditional organizations seek to become more digital, more global, and more agile. Interestingly, the central struggle of the eSports industry is the lack of structures, regulation, and governance. So, there is an interesting paradox to observe. Everybody is moving toward becoming more digital, more global, and more agile, while the eSports industry is moving toward becoming more analog, more regional, and with greater institutionalization. It becomes evident that there is potentially too much digitization, too much globalization, and too much agility. Surprisingly, we can observe a similar trend in other organizations, for example, Tesla, which recently stated that it has too much automation based on an extreme digitizing strategy: the product may be highly globally oriented, but, at the same time, the organization struggles to get the product sold globally, and the agility of Tesla is harming the production processes (Allen 2018). Tesla and the eSports industry highlight that a certain degree of face-to-face interaction (analog), local embedment (regional), and structures (institutionalization) will be necessary to deal with digitization, globalization, and agility. The eSports industry could act as a compelling case for efficiently balancing both worlds, especially as the eSports industry is moving in the opposite direction to most other industries.

Therefore, it will be interesting to describe the eSports phenomenon in detail: it will be analyzed in depth based on various theoretical frameworks rooted in strategic management theory. Especially as the eSports industry is rarely researched from a business perspective, it is necessary to categorize the historical development, the multiple actors and stakeholders involved, the governing principles of the industry, the underlying strategy with a focus on the business model, and a potential look into the future. The following five chapters will give a comprehensive overview of the eSports industry based on appropriate management theories.

In Chap. 2, the history of eSports and management will be presented. As a result of this, the focus lies on an evolutionary perspective of the development from the beginning of competitive gaming. The main focus is on describing the evolution (Darwin 1859) and, by that, explaining the general narrative of eSports. This understanding is essential for the reader to grasp the underlying principles. Every development in the history can be linked to the evolutionary theory of variation, selection, and retention (Aldrich et al. 1984). Even more, eSports sometimes shows a specific form of oblivion and repeats certain mistakes again and again. However, the evolutionary perspective can explain certain developments in the past and, potentially, in the future.

In Chap. 3, the next step after an evolutionary view is identification of the various actors involved in eSports. Thereby, from a strategic management perspective, it seems reasonable to look at the stakeholders involved and how they are involved (Freeman 1984). In particular, the separation of internal and external stakeholders is essential for the analysis of the eSports ecosystem, as many new stakeholders have joined the eSports industry in recent years. What is the position of these stakeholders within the industry and what are the relationships in this environment (Post et al. 2002)? In relation to strategic management, in-depth knowledge is necessary to create a sustainable and profitable business model.

In Chap. 4, the underlying and unwritten principles of the eSports industry will be listed and described in detail. These principles are not derived and propagated by a top-down governing body, but emerged over time through the interaction between actors and stakeholders. Consequently, the creation and diffusion of these principles follow social constructivism (Berger and Luckmann 1966). The various actors in eSports communicated these principles, and through habitualization and repetition, they have become institutionalized, even though they may not be written down in rules or regulations. Depending on the adaptation of other eSports actors, these principles evolved through legitimation by others or were rejected by the eSports community. Based on the long history, some tenets have become apparent and are shared by the eSports community, leading to a certain homogenization, at least in the inner circle of eSports (DiMaggio and Powell 1983).

In Chap. 5, the business model network will be presented, and the interaction of the various business models will be shown. The business model (DaSilva and Trkman 2014) is part of the strategic management of all organizations and can be described as "the rationale of how an organization creates, delivers, and captures value" (Osterwalder and Pigneur 2010, p. 14). Focusing on the business model is essential to have a profitable and potentially sustainable business. Regarding eSports, many stakeholders are heavily intertwined, and cooperation is vital. Depending on others also means that resource allocation needs to stay dynamic, as defined in the dynamic capabilities literature (Eisenhardt and Martin 2000), and any organization will need to balance its exploitation of resources with the exploration of new ideas following the logic of ambidexterity (March 1991).

In Chap. 6, the future of eSports will be tackled. Here, the main focus lies on risk governance (Stein and Wiedemann 2016) and how the eSports industry as a whole and the individual organization can deal with potential risks in eSports' future. Risk governance theory highlights the importance of acknowledging that risks always exist and that it is impossible to minimize risks completely. Risks are interconnected in a risk network, and a good organization can therefore steer its risks sufficiently to gain a competitive advantage from it. Especially in eSports, risk governance will become crucial, as there are many unknown risks that may emerge anytime, but many new opportunities could also emerge. Professional strategic management will proactively search for potential risks to find the next competitive advantage in an industry in which the future is not foreseeable.

References

Aldrich, Howard, Bill McKelvey, and Dave Ulrich. 1984. Design Strategy from the Population Perspective. *Journal of Management* 10 (1): 67–86.

Allen, Tom. 2018. Elon Musk Admits 'Too Much Automation' is Slowing Tesla Model 3 Production. Accessed 2 November 2018. https://www.theinquirer.net/inquirer/news/3030277/elon-musk-admits-too-much-automation-is-slowing-tesla-model-3-production.

Amazon. 2014. Amazon.com to Acquire Twitch. Accessed 2 November 2018. https://web.archive.org/web/20170925163327/http://phx.corporate-ir.net/phoenix.zhtml?c=176060&p=irol-newsArticle&ID=1960768.

Arnaud, Jean-Christophe. 2010. eSports—A New Word. In *eSports Yearbook 2009*, ed. Julia Christophers and Tobias M. Scholz, 11–12. Norderstedt, Germany: Books on Demand.

Bathurst, Eoin. 2017. The Average Age of Esports Viewers is Higher than You May Think, Says GameScape from Interpret, LLC. Accessed 2 November 2018. https://esportsobserver.com/average-age-esports-viewers-gamescape.

Berger, Peter L., and Thomas Luckmann. 1966. *The Social Construction of Reality: A Treatise in the Sociology of Knowledge*. New York: Anchor Books.

Brock, Tom. 2017. Roger Caillois and E-sports: On the Problems of Treating Play as Work. *Games and Culture* 12 (4): 321–339.

Burk, Dan L. 2013. Owning E-Sports: Proprietary Rights in Professional Computer Gaming. *University of Pennsylvania Law Review* 161 (6): 1535–1578.

Byford, Sam. 2014. Twitch Chooses Google over Microsoft amid Multiple Buyout Offers. Accessed 2 November 2018. https://www.theverge.com/2014/5/18/5729762/twitch-youtube-acquisition-report.

Casselmann, Ben. 2015. Resistance is Futile: eSports is Massive … and Growing. Accessed 2 November 2018. http://espn.go.com/espn/story/_/id/13059210/esports-massive-industry-growing.

Chandler, Alfred D. 1962. *Strategy and Structure: Chapters in the History of the American Industrial Enterprise*. Washington, DC: BeardBooks.

Comerford, Sean. 2012. International Intellectual Property Rights and the Future of Global 'E-Sports'. *Brooklyn Journal of International Law* 37 (2): 623–648.

Cunningham, George B., Sheranne Fairley, Lesley Ferkins, Shannon Kerwin, Daniel Lock, Sally Shaw, and Pamela Wicker. 2018. eSport: Construct Specifications and Implications for Sport Management. *Sport Management Review* 21 (1): 1–6.

Darrell, Bracken. 2018. According to Logitech CEO, Esports at the Olympics are 'Inevitable'. Accessed 2 November 2018. https://www.esports.net/logitech-ceo-esports-at-the-olympics/.

Darwin, Charles. 1859. *On the Origin of Species*. London: John Murray.

DaSilva, Carlos M., and Peter Trkman. 2014. Business Model: What It is and What It is Not. *Long Range Planning* 47 (6): 379–389.

DiMaggio, Paul J., and Walter W. Powell. 1983. The Iron Cage Revisited: Institutional Isomorphism and Collective Rationality in Organizational Fields. *American Sociological Review* 48 (2): 147–160.

Drucker, Peter. 1954. *The Practice of Management*. New York: Harper & Row.

Eisenhardt, Kathleen M., and Jeffrey A. Martin. 2000. Dynamic Capabilities: What are They? *Strategic Management Journal* 21 (10–11): 1105–1121.

Freeman, Guo, and Donghee Y. Wohn. 2018. Understanding eSports Team Formation and Coordination. *Computer Supported Cooperative Work* 27 (3–6): 1019–1050.

Freeman, R. Edward. 1984. *Strategic Management: A Stakeholder Approach*. Boston: Pitman.

Funk, Daniel C., Anthondy D. Pizzo, and Bradley J. Baker. 2018. eSport Management: Embracing eSport Education and Research Opportunities. *Sport Management Review* 21 (1): 7–13.

Hetsroni, Amir, and Riva H. Tukachinsky. 2006. Television World Estimates, Real World Estimates, and Television Viewing: A New Scheme for Cultivation. *Journal of Communication* 56 (1): 133–156.

Huizinga, Johan. 1949. *Homo Ludens. A Study of the Play-Element in Culture.* London: Routledge.

Lombardo, John, and David Broughton. 2017. Going Gray. Sports TV Viewers Skew Older. Accessed 2 November 2018. http://www.sportsbusinessdaily. com/Journal/Issues/2017/06/05/Research-and-Ratings/Viewership-trends. aspx.

Newzoo. 2018. *Free 2018 Global Esports Market Report.* Amsterdam: Newzoo.

Nielsen. 2017. *The Esports Playbook. Maximizing Your Investment Through Understanding the Fans.* Cincinnati, OH: Nielsen.

Osterwalder, Alexander, and Yves Pigneur. 2010. *Business Model Generation: A Handbook for Visionaries, Game Changers, and Challengers.* Hoboken, NJ: John Wiley & Sons.

Parshakov, Petr, Dennis Coates, and Marina Zavertiaeva. 2018. Is Diversity Good or Bad? Evidence from eSports Teams Analysis. *Applied Economics* 50 (47): 5064–5075.

Post, James E., Preston Lee, and Sybille Sachs. 2002. Managing the Extended Enterprise: The New Stakeholder View. *California Management Review* 45 (1): 6–28.

Riot. 2017. LoL Esports Events by the Numbers. Accessed 2 November 2018. https://www.lolesports.com/en_US/articles/2017-events-by-the-numbers.

Scholz, Christian. 1987. Corporate Culture and Strategy—The Problem of Strategic Fit. *Long Range Planning* 20 (4): 78–87.

Scholz, Tobias M., and Volker Stein. 2017. Juxtaposing Transduction and Transtraction: Pugging in International Virtual Teams. *Palabra Clave* 20 (3): 788–804.

Schutz, Thomas. 2018. Nerds are Rising: Entwicklung digitaler Führungskompetenz durch Computerspiele wie WoW und LoL. In *Digitale Führungskräfteentwicklung*, ed. Martin A. Ciesielski and Thomas Schutz, 69–84. Berlin and Heidelberg: Springer Gabler.

Seo, Yuri. 2016. Professionalized Consumption and Identity Transformations in the Field of eSports. *Journal of Business Research* 69 (1): 264–272.

Seo, Yuri, and Sang-Uk Jung. 2016. Beyond Solitary Play in Computer Games: The Social Practices of eSports. *Journal of Consumer Culture* 16 (3): 635–655.

Skaugen, Kirk. 2015. The Game Change. Accessed 2 November 2018. https://blogs.intel.com/technology/2015/08/the-game-change.

Stein, Volker, and Tobias M. Scholz. 2016. The Intercultural Challenge of Building the European eSports League for Video Gaming. In *Intercultural Management: A Case-Based Approach to Achieving Complementarity and Synergy*, ed. Christoph Barmeyer and Peter Franklin, 80–94. London: Palgrave Macmillan.

Stein, Volker, and Arnd Wiedemann. 2016. Risk Governance: Conceptualization, Tasks, and Research Agenda. *Journal of Business Economics* 86 (8): 813–836.

Takahashi, Dean. 2015. The Esports Craze Will Generate $1.8B a Year by 2020. Accessed 2 November 2018. http://venturebeat.com/2015/10/05/the-esports-craze-will-generate-1-8b-a-year-by-2020.

Taylor, Nicholas. 2016. Play to the Camera. Video Ethnography, Spectatorship, and E-sports. *Convergence* 22 (2): 115–130.

Teece, David J., Gary Pisano, and Amy Shuen. 1997. Dynamic Capabilities and Strategic Management. *Strategic Management Journal* 18 (7): 509–533.

Wagner, Michael G. 2006. On the Scientific Relevance of eSport. In *Proceedings of the 2006 International Conference on Internet Computing and Conference on Computer Game Development*: 437–440.

Wolf, Jacob. 2018. Tweet. Accessed 2 November 2018. https://www.twitter.com/JacobWolf/status/1020667575661998080.

Wolf, Mark J.P. 2012. *Encyclopedia of Video Games: The Culture, Technology, and Art of Gaming*. Santa Barbara, CA: Greenwood.

2

A Short History of eSports and Management

Abstract The phenomenon of eSports is not a recent development, despite popular opinion being that it emerged just in the last years. The roots of competitive gaming in fact date back to the beginning of computers. Since then, eSports has been part of the evolution of computers and first rose to popularity in the arcade era. With the internet, the current iteration of eSports emerged, and the eSports industry experienced several hypes and crises. Still, there was always space for business, and many existing stakeholders appeared in the early 2000s. The recent years, however, have indeed been a time of exponential growth as well as potential business opportunities.

Keywords eSports • Management history • Emergence • Evolution • Hypes and crises

© The Author(s) 2019
T. M. Scholz, *eSports is Business*, https://doi.org/10.1007/978-3-030-11199-1_2

The Need for a Historical Observation of eSports and Management

Any industry evolves over time and, especially at the beginning of an industry, this evolution can be highly disruptive. Consequently, an organization will evolve with the industry or occasionally disrupt the industry with its innovations. However, strategic management needs to act and react to these developments and plan its course accordingly (Simon 1993). Consequently, there is an evolution of the industry as well as an evolution of the organizations (Nelson and Winter 1982). A prominent theory concerning organizational evolution, the population ecology theory, is derived from Darwin and focuses on the battle for survival (Darwin 1859). Aldrich et al. (1984) applied the variation, selection, and retention/diffusion processes of evolution to organizations. Variation can happen if a new organization is founded or other organizations experience a change. Selection occurs when a fitter organization can create a sustainable strategy and survive, while other less fit organizations vanish. This process will thin out the population in favor of the fitter organizations for this distinct market. Finally, retention or diffusion will preserve the knowledge of the fit organization so that this knowledge can be passed on to the following generations. Market competition will lead to a fierce fight for resources and may lead to an evolutionary race (Hannan and Freeman 1977). "Organizations change over time in one way or another; organizations are created and will potentially die" (Scholz 2017, p. 62). Although this verdict may sound strong, the relevant point is that there is an evolutionary process that goes beyond the organization, and the knowledge in such organizations can be transferred to other organizations within an ecosystem. Consequently, a historical view on eSports is necessary to understand the path eSports took and how the strategic management varied, was selected, and was retained.

Early Years of eSports (1940–1997)

The beginnings of competitive gaming are highly intertwined with the origins of video games, as the first game, *Tennis for Two* from William Higinbotham in 1958, already had a competitive gaming element. It is debatable if *Tennis for Two* was the first game, as the *Nim* game was presented in 1940; yet *Tennis for Two* can be seen as the starting point for the modern video game industry. For *Nim*, competitive gaming was a design element from the beginning, as it was a game where two players competed against each other. Even more, that game was also used as probably the first tournament game, with spectators watching the players. *Nim* was displayed at the New York World's Fair Westinghouse in 1940 (Flesch 1951). The following quotation sounds more like a modern description of an eSports event than an event at a Trade Fair in Berlin in 1951:

> The Germans had never seen anything like it, and came to see it in their thousands, so much so in fact that on the first day of the show they entirely ignored a bar at the far end of the room where free drinks were available, and it was necessary to call out special police to control the crowds. The machine became even more popular after it had defeated the Economics Minister, Dr. Erhardt, in three straight games. (Bowden 1953, p. 287)

Although there was a market for such games, competitions, and tournaments, no business was interested in conquering this untapped market. Nim was just an elaborate demonstration of the technological possibilities, not for entertainment purposes. That is why *Tennis for Two* was so different from every other video game up to then: *Tennis for Two* was created solely for entertainment purposes. The game design already included the spectator as well, as it was possible to follow the match between two players, leading to a public spectacle. At that time, people were already watching other people play video games (Kalning 2008). *Tennis for Two* and other games may have had all the elements of a successful eSports title at that time; however, from a business perspective, it was not feasible to create a video game industry. Computers were expensive and, consequently, there was no market for video games for entertainment purposes. Therefore, until the 1970s, only a small portion of people had access to computers, and those computers were mostly in the workplace.

This changed when computers became cheaper and led to the rise of arcade games and game consoles. Companies like Magnavox, Atari, and Vectorbeam presented their first products around 1972, and the first eSports tournament happened in Stanford in October of that year. The Intergalactic Spacewar Olympics had as its prize a year's subscription to *Rolling Stone* magazine and marked the beginning of a competitive tournament angle to video games (Taylor 2012). In the following years, the market for video games grew, and the number of consoles and arcades rose exponentially. However, many companies involved in these early stages of eSports struggled to monetize their products sufficiently. There were signs, though, that eSports could have had its breakthrough in the early 1980s. The First National Space Invaders in 1980 seemed to be popular, with 10,000 participants and regional qualifiers in Los Angeles, San Francisco, Fort Worth, Chicago, and New York City (Ausretrogamer 2015). Encouraged by the success, Atari announced the World Championships in 1981, with prize money of $50,000. Although between 3000 and 10,000 contestants were expected, only 174 showed up at the event. Players had to finance the whole trip themselves, and that led to poor attendance. In general, the tournament was poorly organized, without specific rules or official referees. Furthermore, it seems that the champions Eric Ginner and Ok-Soo Han never received their prize money. This tournament was, in the end, a fiasco and highlighted the struggle in this era for video games to make a profitable and sustainable business model in arcade games (Smith 2012).

Still, some experiments seemed successful. For example, about 140 episodes were made of the television game show *Starcade* on TBS, in which contestants played against each other (Sheehan 2017). Another innovative idea was the creation of the Twin Galaxies organization. The founder Walter Day created a database of high scores in various arcades. This database became the official scoreboard and helped to organize tournaments and championships (Seppala 2018). Beginning in the 1990s with the Nintendo World Championships, Nintendo utilized tournaments to promote its video games. Consequently, at that time, the business model was focused not on profitability but rather as a marketing tool

(Cifaldi 2015). The arcade era allowed the necessary cultural and economic groundwork for any future development of eSports (Borowy and Jin 2013).

Pioneering eSports (1997–2004)

Due to the personal computer and its affordability for a big part of the society, video games saw further growth in the 1990s. Furthermore, via consoles like the PlayStation, the Game Boy, and others, a broad spectrum of people were now reached by video games. However, competitive gaming had a significant boost due to dedicated multiplayer video games and the possibility of playing them over the internet and at LAN parties. It was now possible to play with other people and have competitions. That change marked a turning point in eSports, where people became able to compete against each other.

This technological and cultural development also led to new business models and new ways to monetize video games. One of the first eSports tournaments was the 1997 Red Annihilation tournament for the video game *Quake*. The prize was the Ferrari 328 GTS owned by the lead developer of the game, John Cormack. Nearly 2000 participants entered the tournament (Adanai 2013). In the following years, several tournament organizations emerged, for example, in the US, the Battle by the Bay (now the Evolution Championship Series) and QuakeCon in 1996 and the Cyberathlete Professional League (CPL) and the AMD Professional Gamers League (PGL) in 1997. In Germany, there was the Deutsche Clanliga (DeCL) in 1997, which became the Electronic Sports League (ESL) in 2000. The competitor for Europe was the Clanbase league, originating in the Netherlands and founded in 1998. Over time, several other tournament operators emerged, like the French Electronic Sports World Cup (ESWC) and US American Major League Gaming (MLG) in 2002. At that time, most of the money for organizing such tournaments came from sponsors: companies like Intel or AMD especially had a keen interest in such competitions. The avid video game player required faster processors, so sponsoring such events was a good marketing investment. However, the business model for eSports was not profitable: the tournament organizers at that time were capable of generating some form of income, but most of that money was reinvested in organizing tournaments. Additionally, the concept of broadcasting was still difficult to handle and not enough bandwidth was available to make a live stream. The solution was complex: in *Counter-Strike*, for example, the viewer had to start the game and join a dedicated spectator server. To hear the commentator, the viewer had to start the audio-stream (or shoutcast). Those two feeds did not sync automatically: the commentator and the viewer had to sync manually. Consequently, only the hardcore fans would join the streams, making it difficult to create a profitable business model for those tournaments. At that time, streaming, and especially video streaming, was not economically viable.

At this time, Asia was struck by a crisis, and South Korea tried to conquer this crisis through modernization. The government subsidized the purchase of a PC and improved internet broadband access. Additionally, so-called PC bangs (internet cafés) became popular (Yoo 2014) as a type of gaming center in which customers could rent a gaming PC to play video games. Based on this development, the infrastructure was perfect for an eSports industry. With the release of *StarCraft* from Blizzard Entertainment, the country became the first powerhouse in eSports, leading to the creation of the Korean e-Sports Association (KeSPA), being part of the Ministry of Culture, Sports and Tourism, the broadcasting of tournaments, a regular league schedule, and an ever-increasing fan base. Furthermore, the South Korean company Samsung funded the World Cyber Games, a global event that was comparable to the Olympic Games. The first actual World Cyber Games had overall prize money of $300,000, and with 430 players from 37 nations, it can be called the first real international eSports tournament (Syrota 2011).

South Korea flourished in those times and had strong governance from the top down at the beginning. It became evident that South Korea would differ from the rest of the world. South Korea was highly controlled and strictly managed, leading to an ecosystem in which business models could evolve (Jin 2010). The rest of the world at that time was the Wild West. Many organizations were founded in those times, and only a few were professional.

A striking example was the Cyber X Games in Las Vegas in 2004. This tournament could have been the biggest tournament ever, with $600,000 in prize money. Sponsors like ATI, AMD, Microsoft, and Sennheiser gave the tournament a professional touch; but in the end it became the biggest fiasco in this eSports era (O'Neill 2012): many tournaments, like the highly anticipated *Counter-Strike* tournament, were canceled, many other tournaments were shut down in the midst of the games, and so on. The tournament was nicknamed the Cancelled X Games and is the worst practice example of terrible tournament organization, scaring off AMD as a sponsor for some time (Gardé 2004). Three months after this disaster, the organizer Chris Hall wrote the following apology (corrected for spelling errors):

> Now most of you hate me and I realize why. Things went wrong, and certain companies didn't do what they promised for us (CXG). This caused total breakdown of CXG. I also take to heart the amount of money and time people wasted preparing for CXG and coming to Las Vegas. It was hard on the community and hard on the players to recover from such a disappointing LAN. I personally feel that things were set up correctly and professionally. (O'Neill 2012)

However, this tournament and other events led to the continual emergence of professionalization in eSports. For example, in 2003, SK Gaming was the first non-Korean organization to have a written contract with one of their players, Ola 'elemeNt' Moum, which was a significant step for SK Gaming and other eSports organizations toward becoming a legitimate business and focusing on their business model. Ola 'elemeNt' Moum achieved another milestone in being the first real transfer in 2004 from SK Gaming to Team NoA (Syrota 2011). Another exciting professionalization development was Alternate (the most prominent online shop for computer hardware in Europe) founding its own corporate team, ALTERNATE aTTaX, in 2003. Besides having a team house, professional support, and regular training sessions, Alternate gave the players the opportunity to participate in vocational training at Alternate (Alternate 2012). The Donau-Universität Krems even offered a Professional E-Sport and Competitive Computer Gaming Master's degree for interested people to prepare their students for an emerging and crucial economic sector (Donau-Universität Krems 2004).

Finally, eSports evolved even further at this time because the video game developers involved themselves in the ecosystem. Although the prize for the first real eSports tournament was the Ferrari belonging to the lead programmer of *Quake*, the game played at that tournament, id Software (the game developer) only partnered up with the actual organizer. At that time, many video game developers did not realize what was happening with their game and did not support the eSports scene, the tournament organizers, or any other institution involved in eSports. Companies like Blizzard regularly worked on the balancing part, but beyond that there was no support at the beginning. Some video games started out as a modification of an existing video game: for example, *Counter-Strike* was created by Minh Le and Jesse Cliffe as a modification of *Half-Life*, and in 2000 *Counter-Strike* was acquired by Valve, the developer of *Half-Life*. This can be seen as a turning point in which video game developers realized the potential of eSports. Although the game itself improved through this acquisition, the spectatorship was still neglected; but in 2001, Valve introduced HLTV, with dedicated servers for streaming *Counter-Strike* matches. After that, more and more video game developers supported the eSports capabilities of their video games.

It is evident that much groundwork was done for the future development of eSports in this era; however, from a business perspective, it was still unclear if this market could grow and become a sustainable business model. At that time, except for South Korea, only a tiny portion of the eSports ecosystem made a profit, and even that profit was quite small. Many people involved in eSports did it for fun and were thrilled to play video games or organize tournaments. Therefore, the primary income in eSports was through sponsoring, and that sponsoring mainly for tournament organizers and the top eSports teams. The eSports teams made some money through the prize money that they had to share with their players. Consequently, tournament organizers who were unprofessional and players who kept losing had to exit the eSports ecosystem and find other jobs. The business model of eSports was at its beginning, but sustainability was not yet achievable.

Experiencing a Phase of Stability (2005–2008)

For the most part, eSports survived the pioneer phase quite well and began to grow steadily. Furthermore, several incidents showed that eSports could become even more prominent. For example, the CPL World Tour was a tournament for the game *Painkiller* and consisted of nine tour stops (Istanbul, Barcelona, Rio de Janeiro, Jönköping, Dallas, Sheffield, Singapore, Milan, and Santiago), culminating in a final tournament in New York City. The prize money was $1,000,000, the largest ever for the CPL. Most importantly, the last game was televised by MTV (Kane 2008). At the same time, the World e-Sports Games were announced, a tournament requiring players to live in China or South Korea. This tournament was the first time that China became active in the international eSports landscape.

Still, many eSports organizations followed their existing business model and tried to grow based on the potential growth of eSports. Several tournament organizers felt the pressure and were unable to create a viable business model. "There was a growing audience for eSports, but no one knew how to make money doing it. Online video via IPTV seemed like a potential solution, considering the close ties video games had with the Internet, but it was expensive and untested, and advertisers didn't understand the medium. Television looked like the only way to leverage the fanbase" (Lingle 2016).

That explains why Turtle Entertainment, the company behind the ESL, acquired the majority rights for NBC GIGA, a television broadcaster with a focus on video games (Lückerath 2005), thereby trying to expand toward linear television to foster growth. Although more and more people had access to an internet flat rate and the internet speed was increasing, the production of content was still expensive for many eSports companies. It seemed that eSports in television, as was already happening in South Korea, might be "the culmination of many dreams that we had of professional gaming" (Munoz, cited in Lingle 2016). Other endeavors included a reality show called *Play Us* in 2005 following the female *Counter-Strike* team Les Seules. MTV tried to make a professional television broadcast happen in the US and started to support the World Series of Video Games (WSVG); later on, the CBS Sports Network took over the role of broadcaster. It seemed that eSports could not be translated into a viable business model on television. At the same time, streaming videos over the internet became increasingly inexpensive, and the eSports ecosystem shifted away from television toward broadcasting solely online. At that time, television was still working well, with a solid business model, and many TV executives did not see the necessity to reach a young audience, sometimes even belittling the eSports organizations. There was no interest, with some exceptions, in broadcasting eSports on a regular basis. Consequently, there was a need to broadcast independently, and many popular eSports commentators emerged in that era (e.g., Nick 'Tasteless' Plott, Marcus 'djWHEAT' Graham, or Thomas 'Khaldor' Kilian). However, eSports was again happening beyond the confines of the living room.

Consequently, failing to monetize through television and online, some eSports organizations vanished. That development struck the US the most, as the CPL had to cease operations in 2008 because the competition was too crowded (Pandey 2008). The WSVG tried to profit from this void in 2006, but could not sustain its business until 2007, again faced by trouble monetizing the tournament, high production costs, and an inappropriate dependency on the sponsors. However, instead of learning the lesson like MLG, which shifted its broadcasting entirely to online streaming, the Championship Gaming Series in 2007 "sowed the seeds of destruction for the North American scene" (Zacny 2016). This league, backed by the satellite broadcast provider DirecTV, started one of the biggest eSports leagues based on the franchise model with city-based teams. To gain reputation and credibility, the CGS tried to recruit as many prominent eSports personalities as possible and even achieve exclusivity by buying brands like CompLexity to become part of its franchise family as Los Angeles Complexity (Lewis 2015). At least in the US, there was no significant competition available: the CPL was gone, the WSVG had failed, and the MLG was focusing more on console games than PC games. Furthermore, the league had $50 million at its disposable and, consequently, money was no problem (O'Neill 2012). This league entered the eSports ecosystem with a big bang, but failed, like many before, to monetize eSports tournaments. Contrary to previously failed tournaments, the CGS dominated the North American scene. This exclusivity was enforced by strict rules that players were not allowed to participate in other tournaments without asking permission from the CGS. Breaking the rules was punished harshly: for example, the player Kevin Wang competed in a different competition and had to pay a $5000 penalty from his salary of $30,000 (Jabzilla 2016). Being promised five years of funding, the league ceased operation in 2008, stating that profitability was not achievable in the short term. In the end, the North American scene was completely devastated after CGS (Li 2017). Jason Lake (owner of CompLexity) summarized the downfall as follows:

> It all went to hell in a hand basket when some well intentioned but corporate suit type people tried to change gaming, the spirit of gaming and it crashed and burned during a bad economy. That was really hard on me, man. I'm quoted on video saying, 'if this doesn't work, eSports is dead' and, unfortunately, I wasn't that far from the truth at the time. When CGS crashed and burned, the scene in North America especially was just a train wreck. That took a lot of emotional energy from me and just sucked it out. (O'Neill 2012)

Outside the North American scene, eSports followed a more organic growth. In Europe, the DreamHack became more popular; the ESWC was a 'must visit' in the tournament schedule for eSports teams; and the WCG traveled outside South Korea, visiting Singapore, Italy, Germany, and China. Additionally, in 2005 the WCG Samsung Euro Championship was founded. The ESL installed the Intel Extreme Masters in 2006 and, unlike the US competition, focused on more gradual and organic growth, expanding slowly over the years. The World e-Sports Games or the World e-Sports Masters moved slowly from South Korea to China, becoming an integral part of the Chinese eSports scene. In South Korea, the growth probably saw its peak around 2005 when the Proleague finals attracted 120,000 people watching the game between SK Telecom T1 and KTF MagicNs in Busan (Korea Joongang Daily 2005). In this year, the player Lim 'BoxeR' Yo-hwan signed a contract with SK Telecom T1 for an annual salary of $180,000 plus up to $80,000 in bonuses (Syrota 2011). All of these cases show that eSports outgrew its business model: some adapted to the new environment, while others failed to change and became extinct.

In addition to these developments, a new generation of eSports organizations emerged, already trying to act like a professional organization from the beginning (e.g., Fnatic or CompLexity). Slow but steady approaches were made to create specific governance structures—for example, federations were founded, culminating in the International e-Sports Federation (IeSf) as an international governing body in 2008. However, they still lacked a certain legitimation from the eSports scene, as well as from other sports federations. Despite several talks, the discussion about eSports as a sport was still ongoing. Also, the aspect of legitimation could be troublesome—for example, the eSports federation in Germany. In 2003, the Deutsche eSport Verband (DeSpV) was founded, and in 2004, the Deutsche eSport Verband e.V. (DeSV) was also founded. After a year of competing against each other, the Deutsche eSport-Bund (ESB) was established; however, since around 2011, this federation has been inactive. Since 2017, the eSport-Bund Deutschland (ESBD) has existed. Although Germany is an extreme example, this case reveals the challenge of creating a professional environment based on a bottom-up approach: besides the KeSPA, no other federation is capable of steering any regulations.

It became apparent that federations may not be the right solution for eSports, and some started to coordinate and create some form of self-regulation. In *Counter-Strike*, for example, the G7 Teams was founded in 2006, consisting of 4Kings, Fnatic, Made in Brazil, Mousesports, NiP, SK Gaming, and Team 3D. The mission was to "promote the cooperation, amicable relations and unity of the member teams" (G7 2007). Although the G7 Teams disbanded due to a dispute between two members, it shaped the mindset that self-regulation was possible and that eSports may find its way regarding governance.

In summary, these years brought some form of stability into eSports and the business model of eSports. It became apparent that the existing business model was too narrow and too volatile. This unviable and unsustainable approach struck the North American scene especially. Even though, in South Korea, eSports was big enough to survive, it reached its peak. The organizations in South Korea, however, focused on their home market and neglected potential internationalization.

Interestingly, the risk-averse approach from the European eSports scene was beneficial at this time. The ESL, with the introduction of the Intel Extreme Masters, filled the void, but, at the same time, the ESL did not overcommit its resources. Furthermore, a certain professionalization was slowly emerging, making these organizations interesting for investment. Those who could show their stability were rewarded with long-term and lucrative sponsorship contracts, allowing a reduction of risks endangering the business. Through experimentation on television and with online media, a broader audience was reachable, but the production costs were still troublesome. The business model, in general, expanded, and there was an increase in revenue streams; at the same time, prices rose. It became apparent that eSports was now business and making a profit was essential for survival.

Phoenix from the Ashes (2009–2013)

Similar to many other industries, the financial crisis had a significant impact on eSports and the companies involved. Primarily due to the fact that eSports was mainly sponsor-driven at that time, everything was downsized (Messier 2011). For example, the WCG 2010 had a prize pool of only $250,000, down from $500,000 in 2009. Crucial sponsors like Nvidia reduced their investment in eSports substantially and stopped sponsoring top events like the ESWC entirely. Matthieu Dallon, founder of the ESWC, explained the reasoning behind this: "[It] is not a secret that all the industries, and notably the ones which traditionally support E-sports, are right now dealing with a global crisis" (Dallon, quoted in Shagrath 2008). In direct consequence, the ESWC did not recover from the loss and filed for bankruptcy in March 2009.

It may be too extreme to say that the eSports bubble burst, but co-aligning with the events in the North American scene, eSports was substantially downsized in that period. However, certain market consolidation and correction were observable, which was comparable to the market cleanup in the financial service sector (Berger et al. 1999). It became evident that the value chain was highly distorted and out of balance; especially, value creation was significantly lacking. This development was observable in the case of the salaries of the *Warcraft III* players, and so in the wake of the financial crisis, teams like SK Gaming or Mousesports exited the *Warcraft III* market, and other organizations like 4Kings and MeetYourMakers vanished because of the struggle to make a profit from the investment in their *Warcraft III* players (Syrota 2011). The financial crisis made it abundantly clear that eSports was too dependent on outside money. The result was that some organizations vanished and others sought to "build our sport on a real, strong base, and to become self-sufficient as an industry" (Messier 2011, p. 55).

The financial crisis led to a shift in mindset, especially as only those people that had already tried to create a sustainable business model survived and stayed in eSports. These years showed that building an audience may be an approach to foster organic growth in eSports by making the games accessible, watchable, enjoyable, and entertaining. As Messier (2011) points out, the solution sounds quite simple. However, eSports had already gambled away its chance with television. Consequently, the internet was the path to success. However, the internet is a difficult market. Transforming or creating a business model in the digital environment proved to be extremely challenging for traditional media. Even the *New York Times*, despite its reputation as a digital role model, has admitted to "not moving with enough urgency" (New York Times 2014, p. 81). Like many legacy media companies, it has not been able to translate its business models into the new digital world effectively (Jenkins 2006) and, consequently, has struggled to survive. This shift can be described as follows: "You are not selling products to the eSports community. What you do sell is emotions. You create a bond between fans, players, organizations, and your brand that if cultivated properly is powerful enough to hold a lifetime" (Franzen, quoted in Li 2017, p. 183).

In the midst of all those turbulent and troublesome times, three events marked a new era in eSports and substantial development: the release of *StarCraft II* in 2010 (or, more accurately, the announcement of that game), the release of *League of Legends* in 2009, and the founding of Twitch in 2011. All three events helped to shake off the lethargy of recent years and create a momentum that, contrary to previous hype phases, many eSports organizations could translate into a sustainable business model. These events allowed eSports to grow into a business that could focus on steady revenue streams, steady and less risky growth, and subsequently sustainable business models.

There were some things that could drive video gamers to create a momentum that businesses could utilize for their business model, especially in the late 2000s. One was the announcement of *Half-Life 3*; another was a video of a soldier in a specific sci-fi setting. In May 2007, at the Worldwide Invitational Tournament from Blizzard Entertainment in Seoul, this soldier said in a trailer "Hell, it's about time". The audience "freaked out" (Li 2017, p. 52), as with this trailer, *StarCraft II* was announced. Blizzard would still work on the game for the next three years, but even in the Beta stages, people played the game, players joined eSports teams, professional players moved from the traditional *StarCraft* and from *Warcraft III* to the new game, and tournaments were organized. This was unprecedented at the time, as usually an eSports scene evolved after the release and, at least, acted as a form of rallying cry for the eSports scene and revitalized many eSports people. *StarCraft II* helped eSports fundamentally; however, the game itself quickly began to struggle (Partin 2018a).

Although the multiplayer online battle arena (MOBA) genre was invented in 2003 with the *Defense of the Ancients* (*DotA*) modification of *Warcraft III*, the genre gained real popularity with the release of *League of Legends* in 2009. *DotA* heavily inspired the game, but, in contrast to many games, there was strong developer support. In particular, the changes every two weeks and the constant addition of new heroes were unseen at time (Riot n.d.). That kept the game fresh and entertaining for the players. Over the years, Riot Games, the developer, supported the eSports scene by making the game more spectator friendly and organizing the first World Championship in 2011. Later, in 2012 and 2013, Riot went even further and created the League of Legends Championship Series (LCS) (theScore 2017). Backed by Riot Games, this league system brought stability to the eSports scene, and eSports organizations could build a sustainable business model around this game. It even meant that pro-players had a chance to have a fixed salary; however, the league was still faced with an annual roster shuffle (ESPN 2017). Besides creating developer-driven structures in that case, Riot Games shared its growth with the eSports industry, and many new eSports organizations emerged in that time. Furthermore, the MOBA genre became so popular that Valve released *Dota 2* in 2013 and Blizzard Entertainment *Heroes of the Storm* in 2015.

The next significant development evolved into a crucial cornerstone that will be essential for the growth of eSports in the coming years. At that time, eSports was still struggling to reach its audience: a few people visited the tournaments, others mastered the difficulties of watching the games online; but there was no easy way to watch the games. That changed with Justin.tv, a platform introduced in 2007, at that time with a focus on broadcasting live content. In the following years, it became evident that video games were the most prominent content streamed on Justin.tv, so they announced the gaming division Twitch in 2013 (Taylor 2018). The principal competitive advantage was the easiness of streaming: anybody could stream, and consequently, streaming or IPTV grew exponentially (Scholz 2012). Alongside tournament organizers utilizing Twitch, suddenly professional eSports players could broadcast their training and create other events (Scholz and Stein 2017). The aspect of streaming became a steady revenue stream for professional players, and for some players it can account for a third of their annual income. Twitch became a stabilizing factor for eSports; additionally, it showed the world what was happening. People were now able to watch any tournament easily and, besides the benefit of having growing spectatorship, eSports organizations became able to show their value creation in specific numbers. "The current esports boom began in part because Twitch offered a suite of viewing metrics that made it much easier for esports teams and tournaments to negotiate with sponsors. In turn, the growth of esports normalized the practice of watching video games. Twitch and esports have been intertwined for nearly a decade, and the vibrant esports landscape we have is unthinkable without their symbiosis" (Partin 2018b).

Based on these developments, there was an observable steady growth in eSports, and other games had to adapt to the new situation. A striking example is *Counter-Strike*, especially as the *Counter-Strike* scene was separated into people playing *Counter-Strike 1.6* and those playing *Counter-Strike: Source*. There was an ongoing debate over which game was better;

however, ultimately, it meant that people had to choose. From the people perspective, two similar games had to compete for players, teams, tournaments, and, finally, the audience. It was the first time that a cannibalization effect was observable, and both scenes started to stagnate or, as Nathan Schmitt summarized, "We have milked CS 1.6 and CSS empty" (Schmitt, quoted in Dchozn 2012). The developer Valve realized the struggle and in 2012 released another iteration of the game called *Counter-Strike: GO*. It was a risky move, as the game design may not be the deciding factor for these separated audiences; especially, uniting two communities divided by the game design topic may be extremely difficult. Interestingly, this challenge was observed by the community itself, and *Counter-Strike: GO* was able to unify both communities. The best players of both games joined together and the audience no longer had to choose. The two fractured communities were now once again unified (Gonzales 2017), especially as Valve was now actively involved in supporting the *Counter-Strike* community—for example, the introduction of so-called arms deals, a way to get weapon skins in game, and a portion of all sales put into the prize pool for upcoming events (Mitchell 2018). This led to a development through which *Counter-Strike* emerged like a phoenix and was reborn.

This short period highlighted the cleansing effect of the financial crisis and the focus on a core aspect of the eSports business model, the audience. Supported by the technological progress in live streaming through Twitch, anyone was now able to reach their audience, a development that helped to conquer new markets and create a steady revenue stream for eSports organizations. The business model became plannable, and it was possible to make strategic decisions beyond the one-year time frame. Consequently, the business model moved from being purely sponsor-driven to being audience-focused. Equipped with metrics and numbers, it was possible to attract new sponsors and show them their return on investment. Although the growth in that period was not exponential, it was organic and less risky. The scene may not be flooded with money (Li 2017), but it was possible to make a sustainable business model, and more players could become full-time professionals. Furthermore, the developers finally realized the potential of eSports and included the eSports title in their business model. Companies like Riot Games understood it well and created a league system around their game. These developments show the first tendencies of the eSports business model network in which every stakeholder is highly intertwined with other stakeholders to reach the audience and make a profit from the audience. All this culminated in the situation that "eSports are suddenly the golden goose everyone is chasing" (Popper 2013).

Back to the Wild West (Since 2014)

Based on the exponential growth, it was understandable that bigger companies may become interested in eSports and, as mentioned above, the acquisition of Twitch by Amazon led to a buying frenzy that continues today. More and more companies from outside the endemic eSports ecosystem are becoming interested in eSports and are shaping the business model network we can observe today. The development in this era is the basis of the ongoing in-depth research into actors and stakeholders, as well as the business model network. The evolution of eSports and these newcomers also influenced the unwritten principles that govern the current eSports industry.

However, there are some crucial developments that it is necessary to highlight—for example, the installation of the annual *Dota 2* tournament, The International, in 2011. The tournament gained significant attention, not only being organized by the developer Valve, but having a $1.6 million prize pool, awarding the winning team a staggering $1 million. The event introduced a fundraising element, comparable to the *Counter-Strike* concept, for the prize pool. The audience could buy a digital compendium, and the profit from that was added to the prize pool. This compendium gave the buyer information about the event and the teams, let them play against other viewers, provided them with the chance of special in-game item drops, let them vote for the tournament awards, and allowed predictions. Most importantly, 25% of the $10 cost of the compendium went into the prize pool (Gera 2014). The latest installment in 2018 amounted to over $25 million, and with a base prize pool of $1,600,000 from Valve, the community donated nearly $24 million. Another relevant tournament organizer was established in 2016, filling the void in North America. The ELEAGUE was initiated by the media company Turner and was broadcast on both TBS and Twitch. The main focus was on *Counter-Strike*, and it became an essential tournament for *Counter-Strike* with solid viewership numbers, TBS eSports playing a vital role in the revamp of the network (Dave 2015).

Even though there was ongoing hype, not everybody was successful and could adapt their business model. The prestigious World Cyber Games were shut down in 2014, making it again blatantly clear that a sustainable business model is necessary to minimize potential risks. The former WCG organizer Lin Yuxin explained that the WCG lost Samsung as the primary sponsor due to a shift in Samsung's strategy toward mobile products (Yuxin, cited in Custer 2014). Furthermore, WCG failed to diversify its business model in the years it grew and flourished. Finally, the Olympic concept is extraordinarily expensive in smaller and underdeveloped countries, so, in the end, the WCG had a terrible business model solely relying on Samsung, and without Samsung, the WCG crumbled.

Another struggling organization in eSports is Blizzard Entertainment. Although with *StarCraft* it had the primary driver of eSports in South Korea and, with *Warcraft III*, the rest of the world, Blizzard Entertainment was mostly acting as a game developer supporting eSports. With the StarCraft II World Championship Series, it joined the tournament circle; however, it was not able to keep up the momentum and after two years the numbers plummeted (Partin 2018a). South Korea dominated the world; at the same time, the Korean market was divided into *StarCraft* and *StarCraft II*. There was no competition for *StarCraft II*, but it degenerated into a niche game. The developer ventured into the MOBA sector with Heroes of the Storm, and despite the fourth highest prize money, the game still struggles (Pickard 2018). Even the successful game *World of Warcraft* is not well received in the eSports sector, and recent successes have been without any support from the developer (Cocke 2018). The card game *Hearthstone* has a small but loyal eSports audience, but can only be seen as a niche game in eSports. These developments show a track record of Blizzard being outstanding in creating a niche game complementing other more prominent titles. That may have changed with *Overwatch*, but this case requires a more detailed description later on in this book. However, it seems that Blizzard Entertainment is heavily invested in *Overwatch* and is moving employees away from other games (Mitrevski 2017).

Also, recent years have shown some efforts to create regulations and governance structures by installing the Esports Integrity Coalition in 2016, introducing doping controls, and fighting against match-fixing. In South Korea, some professional players involved in match-fixing were sentenced to jail. Furthermore, the World Esports Association (WESA) was founded to foster rules and regulations. Unions in *League of Legends*, *Overwatch*, and *Counter-Strike* emerged, although only the Counter-Strike Professional Players' Association (CSPPA) seemed to be created by the players themselves: in *League of Legends*, the union was enabled by Riot Games, while the *Overwatch* union went silent with the inaugural Overwatch League season (Locklear 2018).

Some turmoil came with the explosion of popularity for Battle Royale games like *PlayerUnknown's Battlegrounds* (*PUBG*) and *Fortnite*. Epic Games, the developer of *Fortnite*, especially revealed their keen interest in eSports with the revelation of a $100 million prize pool for the first year of *Fortnite* eSports (Donnelly 2018). Although most of the Battle Royale games are not eSports ready at the competitive level (Van Allen 2017; Bycer 2018), the potential is massive. The competition *PUBG* even states that the game is not eSports ready (Jones 2018), but its first tournament in July 2018 already showed a high production value (Wells 2018).

The eSports history is not yet finished, and even in the time this book is being written more and more stories will evolve. It is important to highlight that eSports is highly dynamic and that new actors join the industry on a daily basis. It is necessary to have a closer look at the actors and stakeholders, as well as the business model network that connects everybody in the eSports scene. There are some profitable ways to create a revenue stream, but there is still a certain volatility. Just copying best practices does not work in eSports. Consequently, strategic management will be essential to achieve competitive advantage. However, learning from the mistakes in the history will be helpful, and there are ways potentially to minimize the risk of failure and increase the profitability of the business model. An overview of the actors, the underlying principles, the business model network, and the potential future of eSports will be presented in the following chapters.

References

Adanai. 2013. Esports: A Brief History. Accessed 2 Nov adanai.com/esports.

Aldrich, Howard, Bill McKelvey, and Dave Ulrich. 1984. Desig. the Population Perspective. *Journal of Management* 10 (1): 67–86.

Alternate. 2012. ALTERNATE aTTaX!—ALTERNATE sein eSport-Clan. Accessed 2 November 2018. https://blog.alternate.de/2012/07/10/alternate-attax-alternate-und-sein-esport-clan.

Ausretrogamer. 2015. The Atari $50,000 World Championships Fiasco. Accessed 2 November 2018. http://www.ausretrogamer.com/tag/1980s-gaming-tournaments.

Berger, Allen N., Rebecca S. Demsetz, and Philip E. Strahan. 1999. The Consolidation of the Financial Services Industry: Causes, Consequences, and Implications for the Future. *Journal of Banking & Finance* 23 (2–4): 135–194.

Borowy, Michael, and Dal Yong Jin. 2013. Pioneering eSport: The Experience Economy and the Marketing of Early 1980s Arcade Gaming Contests. *International Journal of Communication* 7: 2254–2274.

Bowden, B.V. 1953. *Faster than Thought. A Symposium on Digital Computing Machines*. London: Sir Isaac Pitman & Sons.

Bycer, Josh. 2018. Is Battle Royale the Next Esport? Accessed 2 November 2018. https://www.gamasutra.com/blogs/JoshBycer/20180615/320045/Is_Battle_Royale_the_Next_Esport.php.

Cifaldi, Frank. 2015. The Story of the First Nintendo World Championships. Accessed 2 November 2018. https://www.ign.com/articles/2015/05/13/the-story-of-the-first-nintendo-world-championships.

Cocke, Taylor. 2018. Method's World of Warcraft Raid Race Uncovers Untapped Esports Market. Accessed 2 November 2018. https://esportsobserver.com/method-wow-untapped-market.

Custer, C. 2014. Why the World Cyber Games Got Cancelled: It's All Samsung's Fault. Accessed 2 November 2018. https://www.techinasia.com/why-the-world-cyber-games-got-cancelled-its-all-samsungs-fault.

Darwin, Charles. 1859. *On the Origin of Species*. London: John Murray.

Dave, Paresh. 2015. Competitive Video Gaming is Set to Return to TV in 2016. Accessed 2 November 2018. http://www.latimes.com/business/la-fi-turner-img-esports-20150924-story.html.

ıozn. 2012. NBK: 'We Have Milked CS 1.6 and CSS Empty'. Accessed 2 November 2018. https://play.esea.net/index.php?s=news&d=content &id=11446.

Donau-Universität Krems. 2004. Der Computer als Sportgerät. Accessed 2 November 2018. https://www.donau-uni.ac.at/de/aktuell/presse/ archiv/03317.

Donnelly, Joe 2018. Epic to Provide $100 Million Prize Pool for First Year of Fortnite Esports Tournaments. Accessed 2 November 2018. https://www. pcgamer.com/epic-to-provide-dollar100-million-prize-pool-for-first-year-of-fortnite-esports-tournaments.

ESPN. 2017. The 2017–2018 League of Legends Roster Shuffle. Accessed 2 November 2018. http://www.espn.com/esports/story/_/id/18107525/the-2017-2018-league-legends-roster-shuffle.

Flesch, Rudolf. 1951. *The Art of Clear Thinking*. New York: Harper and Brothers Publishers.

G7. 2007. Mission Statement. Accessed 2 November 2018. https://web.archive. org/web/20070124100245/http://www.g7teams.com.

Gardé, Etienne. 2004. Die Cyber X Games—Die Ganze Wahrheit über den Flop Event des Jahres. Accessed 2 November 2018. https://www.giga-search. de/0,3404,75873,00.html.

Gera, Emily. 2014. What is the Dota 2 Compendium. Accessed 2 November 2018. https://www.polygon.com/2014/7/16/5898483/what-is-the-dota-2-compendium.

Gonzales, Dennis. 2017. The Rise, Fall, and Rise Again of Chinese Counter-Strike. Accessed 2 November 2018. https://www.thescoreesports.com/csgo/ news/13976-the-rise-fall-and-rise-again-of-chinese-counter-strike.

Hannan, Michael T., and John Freeman. 1977. The Population Ecology of Organizations. *American Journal of Sociology* 82 (5): 929–964.

Jabzilla. 2016. History of Counter Strike: The CGS Years. Accessed 2 November 2018. https://www.hltv.org/blog/12903/history-of-counter-strike-the-cgs-years.

Jenkins, Henry. 2006. *Convergence Culture: Where Old and New Media Collide*. New York: New York University Press.

Jin, Dal Yong. 2010. *Korea's Online Gaming Empire*. Cambridge, MA: MIT Press.

Jones, Ali. 2018. PUBG Creator Says 'We're Not Esports Ready' at PUBG Global Invitational. Accessed 2 November 2018. https://www.pcgamesn. com/playerunknowns-battlegrounds/pubg-esports-ready.

Kalning, Kristin. 2008. The Anatomy of the First Video Game. Accessed 2 November 2018. http://www.nbcnews.com/id/27328345.

Kane, Michael. 2008. *Game Boys: Triumph, Heartbreak, and the Quest for Cash in the Battleground of Competitive Videogaming*. New York: Plume.

Korea Joongang Daily. 2005. StarCraft Finals Draw Crowds to Busan Beach. Accessed 2 November 2018. http://koreajoongangdaily.joins.com/news/article/article.aspx?aid=2600715.

Lewis, Richard. 2015. Echoes of Future Past: The Ghost of the CGS and What It Means for Counter-Strike. Accessed 2 November 2018. https://dotesports.com/counter-strike/news/cgs-vulcun-twitch-esl-counter-strike-league-1665.

Li, Roland. 2017. *Good Luck Have Fun: The Rise of Esports*. New York: Skyhorse.

Lingle, Samuel. 2016. The Complicated Past (and Future) of Esports on TV. Accessed 2 November 2018. https://kernelmag.dailydot.com/issue-sections/headline-story/16083/eleague-esports-tv-history.

Locklear, Mallory. 2018. Two Major eSports Players Associations are in the Works. Accessed 2 November 2018. https://www.engadget.com/2018/03/15/overwatch-counter-strike-players-associations-in-the-works.

Lückerath, Thomas. 2005. NBC Universal gibt Mehrheit an GIGA Digital Television ab. Accessed 2 November 2018. https://www.dwdl.de/nachrichten/5722/nbc_universal_gibt_mehrheit_an_giga_digital_television_ab.

Messier, Marc-Andre. 2011. The Lessons eSports Should Learn from the Recession. In *eSports Yearbook 2010*, edited by Julia Christophers and Tobias M. Scholz, 54–60. Norderstedt, Germany: Books on Demand.

Mitchell, Ferguson. 2018. Esports Essentials: The Impact of the Counter-Strike Majors. Accessed 2 November 2018. https://esportsobserver.com/esports-essentials-counter-strike-majors.

Mitrevski, Lydia. 2017. Why Don't Esports Organisations Care About Heroes of the Storm? Accessed 2 November 2018. https://www.mcvuk.com/esportspro/why-dont-esports-organisations-care-about-heroes-of-the-storm.

Nelson, Richard R., and Sidney G. Winter. 1982. The Schumpeterian Tradeoff Revisited. *American Economic Review* 72 (1): 114–132.

New York Times. 2014. *Innovation Report*. New York: New York Times.

O'Neill, Patrick H. 2012. A History of Esports. Accessed 2 November 2018. https://github.com/hubwub/history-of-esports.

Pandey, Rohan. 2008. Cyberathlete Professional League (CPL) is No More! Accessed 2 November 2018. http://www.gameguru.in/pc/2008/17/cyberathlete-professional-league-cpl-is-no-more.

Partin, Will. 2018a. 'StarCraft II': How Blizzard Brought the King of Esports Back From the Dead. Accessed 2 November 2018. https://variety.com/2018/gaming/features/StarCraft-ii-esports-history-1202873246.

———. 2018b. Twitch Isn't for Esports. It's for Streamers. Accessed 2 November 2018. https://compete.kotaku.com/twitch-isnt-for-esports-its-for-streamers-1824263773.

Pickard, James. 2018. The Rise and Fall and Rise Again of Heroes of the Storm Esports. Accessed 2 November 2018. https://www.rockpapershotgun.com/2018/08/17/the-rise-and-fall-and-rise-again-of-heroes-of-the-storm-esports.

Popper, Ben. 2013. Field of Streams: How Twitch Made Video Games a Spectator Sport. Accessed 2 November 2018. https://www.theverge.com/2013/9/30/4719766/twitch-raises-20-million-esports-market-booming.

Riot. n.d. Accessed 2 November 2018. https://na.leagueoflegends.com/en/news/game-updates.

Scholz, Tobias M. 2012. New Broadcasting Ways in IPTV—The Case of the Starcraft Broadcasting Scene. Paper presented at the World Media Economics & Management Conference in Thessaloniki, Greece.

———. 2017. *Big Data in Organizations and the Role of Human Resource Management*. Frankfurt am Main: Peter Lang.

Scholz, Tobias M., and Volker Stein. 2017. Going Beyond Ambidexterity in the Media Industry: eSports as Pioneer of Ultradexterity. *International Journal of Gaming and Computer-Mediated Simulations* 9 (2): 47–62.

Seppala, Timothy J. 2018. Video Game Records are Broken. Can Anyone Fix Them? Accessed 2 November 2018. https://www.engadget.com/2018/02/14/twin-galaxies-donkey-kong-dragster-records.

Shagrath. 2008. Nvidia and ESWC Part Company. Accessed 2 November 2018. http://www.sk-gaming.com/content/20612-Nvidia_and_ESWC_part_company.

Sheehan, Gavin. 2017. A Look Back at the Show 'Starcade' With the Creators. Accessed 2 November 2018. https://www.bleedingcool.com/2017/09/12/a-look-back-at-starcade-with-the-creators.

Simon, Herbert A. 1993. Strategy and Organizational Evolution. *Strategic Management Journal* 14 (S2): 131–142.

Smith, Keith. 2012. The Atari $50,000 Centipede Fiasco. Accessed 2 November 2018. http://allincolorforaquarter.blogspot.com/2012/11/the-atari-50000-centipede-fiasco.html.

Syrota, Lari. 2011. eSports. A Short History of Nearly Everything. Accessed 2 November 2018. https://www.teamliquid.net/forum/starcraft-2/249860-esports-a-short-history-of-nearly-everything.

Taylor, T.L. 2012. *Raising the Stakes: E-sports and the Professionalization of Computer Gaming.* Cambridge, MA: MIT Press.

———. 2018. *Watch Me Play. Twitch and the Rise of Game Live Streaming.* Princeton, NJ and Oxford: Princeton University Press.

theScore. 2017. Infographic: The History of League of Legends. Accessed 2 November 2018. https://www.thescoreesports.com/lol/news/14525-infographic-the-history-of-league-of-legends.

Van Allen, Eric. 2017. Battle Royale Esports are Still a Work in Progress. Accessed 2 November 2018. https://compete.kotaku.com/battle-royale-esports-are-still-a-work-in-progress-1794707007.

Wells, Jessica. 2018. PUBG's Global Invitational Proved That Battle Royale Esports are Here to Stay. Accessed 2 November 2018. https://www.pcgamesn.com/playerunknowns-battlegrounds/pubg-global-invitational-tpp-finals.

Yoo, Reera. 2014. How 'E-Sports' Outgrew 'Real Sports' in South Korea. Accessed 2 November 2018. http://kore.am/how-esports-outgrew-real-sports-in-south-korea.

Zacny, Rob. 2016. The Continental Counter-Strike Divide. Accessed 2 November 2018. https://www.redbull.com/us-en/the-continental-counter-strike-divide.

3

Stakeholders in the eSports Industry

Abstract The eSports industry is a multifaceted industry involving many different stakeholders, all of them contributing to the value chain or the value integration of the audience that is experiencing the various eSports products. Notably, the long-term stakeholders in eSports are highly intertwined and interconnected, creating a business around the audience. Based on the long-term relationships, certain essential eSports characteristics emerge that explain parts of the behavior of these primary stakeholders. In recent years, various secondary stakeholders joined this industry with different industry backgrounds. They have introduced new ideas and new concepts, but are trying to find their place in the stakeholder network of eSports. Consequently, defining the primary and secondary stakeholders is necessary.

Keywords eSports • eSports industry • Stakeholder analysis • Strategic management • eSports characteristics

A Stakeholder Journey Through the eSports Industry

Although the eSports industry is currently hyped and some industry reports state that the revenue will explode in the coming years—for example, Berenberg noted that the revenue would rise to $20 billion in 2025 (Rosa 2018)—the underlying industry has evolved slowly over time. As stated in the previous chapter, many actors are involved for decades. Some of the biggest names have their roots in the early 2000s. Furthermore, it is becoming evident that eSports is a complex and highly interwoven system. Many of the actors depend on each other: without an eSports title, no tournaments; without tournaments, no teams; and without teams, no audience that can cheer—or, in business terms, be monetized. The interconnection is relevant for an analysis of the eSports industry, as the focus is mainly on the stakeholders involved in eSports. Stakeholders can be defined as "groups without whose support the organization would cease to exist" (Freeman and Reed 1983, p. 89).

In this book, the stakeholder journey will be applied to map the several stakeholders involved in the eSports industry to give insights into this emerging industry. A stakeholder analysis is often used in connection with organizations, but can also be applied to industry-level research. Furthermore, a stakeholder analysis is commonly used to understand the behavior of the stakeholders. This understanding is relevant to a volatile industry like eSports (Brugha and Varvasovszky 2000). Although the borders of organizations in eSports are sometimes opaque, a focus on the internal and external stakeholders within an organization and within the industry could be a competitive advantage for any organization involved in eSports (Savage et al. 1991). Therefore, identifying and understanding the role of every stakeholder in this network will be necessary for any organization to survive and thrive (Bryson 2004).

It becomes evident that any stakeholder is relevant to the success of an organization. Freeman describes a stakeholder as "any group or individual who can affect or is affected by the achievement of the organization's objectives" (Freeman 1984, p. 46). However, for any organization, categorization is necessary to reduce complexity; therefore, there are primary and secondary stakeholders. Darnall et al. (2010) describe primary stakeholders as value chain stakeholders who have a direct impact and who will, additionally, interact with the internal stakeholders. Secondary stakeholders have an indirect effect and are often seen as environmental or societal stakeholders (Darnall et al. 2010). In eSports, there are also two types of stakeholder. Primary stakeholders are linked in the value chain or the value chain network and need each other, at least to a certain degree. This type includes the key stakeholder, the audience, that everybody is fighting for and trying to monetize. Secondary stakeholders have an indirect influence and impact on the eSports industry. They are not directly linked to the value chain, but influence the primary stakeholders through investment, opinions, and regulations. Primary stakeholders have to respond to the actions of secondary stakeholders and categorize the power, legitimacy, and urgency of these secondary stakeholders (Eesley and Lenox 2006).

As depicted in Fig. 3.1, the primary stakeholders try to interact with the critical stakeholder audience. They can be separated further based on their position in the value network and can be categorized based on Porter's value chain logic (Porter 1985). Game developers, professional teams, tournament organizers, and professional players are primary roles that are essential for the eSports industry. The primary stakeholders' service providers, communities, hardware providers, and infrastructure providers are support activities. The secondary stakeholders—governing bodies, sports businesses, sponsors, the general public, investors, entrepreneurs, media businesses, and shareholders—do not contribute directly to the value chain network, but influence the eSports industry heavily through investments or pressure for change in a particular direction. All of these stakeholders have specific needs (Ballantyne et al. 2013), expectations (Fletcher et al. 2003), interests (Reynolds et al. 2006), and politics (Freeman 1994).

Fundamental Characteristics of eSports Stakeholders

In order to get a more precise understanding of the stakeholders involved in eSports, it is essential to describe certain fundamental characteristics. These characteristics are predominantly found in primary stakeholders, but some successful secondary stakeholders try to adapt to these charac-

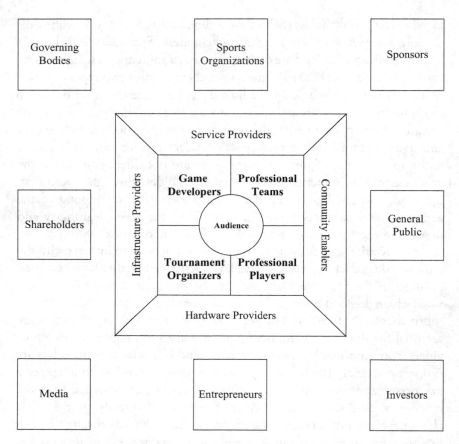

Fig. 3.1 Primary and secondary stakeholders in the eSports industry

teristics. As stated above, the eSports industry evolved without much interference from other actors and organizations. Many organizations that learned to adapt became long-term stakeholders, like Intel. Intel nowadays goes beyond being a sponsor and is rather an advocate and ambassador for eSports. It is part of the eSports community. The Championship Gaming Series is a typical example of outside organizations trying to enforce their rules on eSports, which ended in disaster, especially for the North American eSports scene (Taylor 2018).

Most of the stakeholders evolved from within, and many early eSports organizations emerged from people solely interested in playing games competitively. This first generation of eSports organizations had the chance to evolve without much interference from other organizations that may have an interest in doing business in eSports. This unique situation in an industry can be ascribed to the fact that eSports is difficult to measure in traditional business terms. Especially in the early 2000s, many organizations were struggling to find investors or sponsors, primarily because they were not able to show reliable numbers to prove their success (Cocke 2018a). Consequently, only a certain type of organization got involved in eSports in the beginning, allowing this 'inner circle' of enthusiasts to evolve on their own and create distinct characteristics. Moreover, there was enough time to create a certain cultural understanding; it may even be the case that the eSports industry is in a lock-in in terms of these cultural similarities, which may be difficult for outsiders to grasp, especially as they evolved globally and are shared by many stakeholders. Therefore, to understand the eSports industry in its current evolution, Scholz and Stein (2017) distinguished the eSports actors according to six fundamental characteristics.

- *The people involved with eSports are highly focused on goal setting.* Teams, for example, want to be the best at a particular game or to deliver the best possible experience for their fans and their viewers. That is why they constantly seek new ideas and concepts for the sake of improvement. Their pursuit is not limited to radical innovations, but also includes minor process innovations. Any change for the better is utilized and can be employed to move closer to those ambitious goals.
- *The market's orientation is truly glocal.* Glocal refers to the idea that a company thinks global and acts local (Svensson 2001). This characteristic may come as a surprise given that eSports originally started out as a virtual product (Weiss and Schiele 2013), but eSports events fill entire stadiums like Madison Square Garden in New York City and Wembley Arena in London (Thompson 2015). Simultaneously, hundreds of thousands or even millions of people may be watching a tournament live on the internet. eSports companies are positioned in both worlds, and it seems to pay off.

- *eSports are oriented toward change.* It seems only natural for participants in eSports media to seek change and to be passionate about it (Weststar 2015). A strategy of trial and error is commonly employed (Scholz 2015), and this approach is linked to the tenacity required to keep changing until success is achieved. Players and companies change and redefine themselves until they find the right path. When an innovation is deemed to be successful, it is exploited to the fullest. Exploitation and exploration therefore occur simultaneously.
- *Resources are allocated in a bottom-up fashion.* The allocation of resources in eSports has always taken place in a bottom-up manner. Throughout the beginning stages of the internet, connections were poor and network resources had to be allocated judiciously. It was important, then, that any progress in technology was employed to improve the infrastructure supporting gaming. In addition to these technical obstacles, resources were scarce and there was no governing unit with the authority to compel individual actors to contribute in ways that produced collective benefits. Instead, there was a decentralized network of actors who used and contributed their own resources in ways that all benefitted from. This approach prevails in the eSports media sphere to this day, and the eSports business model network still has no dominant central authority.
- *Participants are over-energetic, over-enthusiastic, and over-dynamic.* As mentioned above, the enthusiasm of actors within the eSports media sphere is one of its key characteristics. These traits can be linked to the idea of the entrepreneurial innovator (Gray 1978). Entrepreneurial innovators intend to prove their capabilities by their "over-energetic, over-enthusiastic, over-dynamic" (Gray 1978, p. 88) nature. The eSports media sphere is filled with actors driven by passion and dedication (Giannacco 2015). This refers to all actors—and customers are no exception. Franke (2015, p. 139) states that "what makes eSports so valuable for marketing is the level of involvement of consumers with the product". The dynamism in eSports is a reflection of the people involved.
- *Digitization is integral to eSports.* Due to eSports' digital nature and the general alignment of its growth with the growth of the internet, this may not come as a surprise. But the impact of digitization goes further, leading to the formation of virtual teams all over the world. Key organizations—including teams, tournament operators, infrastructure

providers, and communities—can exist virtually and in a decentralized fashion (Stein and Scholz 2016). Virtual collaboration may not be out of the ordinary today, but everybody in eSports has worked together in virtual collaboration since the early 2000s.

All these characteristics contribute to a fascinating momentum and a distinctive and shared understanding of the eSports media sphere. Scholz and Stein (2017) describe this as entrepreneurial innovativeness and dynamic commitment. Companies located within the eSports industry have a completely different understanding of the way organizations work. People are committed to their companies as well as to the overarching eSports industry. They willingly commit and aspire to improve their operations on the organizational level, but concern themselves with the future of eSports at the network level as well. However, for newly joining organizations, the situation will lead to an initial tension between characteristics. On the one hand, there are new actors that accept the shared values, like Rick Fox, former NBA player and now owner of the eSports team Echo Fox, who puts it as follows: "Outside of cheering for Echo Fox, I cheer for the eSports space as a whole. In most cases, what is good for one team is good for all teams" (Fox, quoted in Volk 2016). On the other hand, there are other actors like the International Olympic Committee (IOC) that recently demanded a recognized international federation for eSports to be considered as an Olympic discipline (Williams 2018). As this industry is gathering interest in 'traditional' organizations like media or sports, this tension or clash will influence the development of eSports in the future.

Primary Stakeholders

Game Developer

The game developer is probably the most crucial stakeholder, as he is creating the eSports title everybody is playing. Consequently, the whole eSports value chain or the eSports experience for the audience is built around a dedicated video game with potential as an eSports title. Many modern video games have some form of competition mode and allow players to play against each other, but not all video games are capable of being an eSports title. Competition should be balanced, and it should be fun to watch. Beyond that, many eSports titles are updated continuously, and new content will be administered on a regular basis. For example, *League of Legends* updates the game every two weeks (Riot n.d.).

This ongoing updating has led to a shift in the game developer mindset. Especially in the early 2000s, many game developers did not realize their impact, and some did not care about it. Use of the games as eSports titles was a simple way to enhance the lifespan of their video games: beyond that, it had only a marginal impact on their strategy. The success of *StarCraft* in South Korea surprised Blizzard Entertainment (Reimer 2011), and *Counter-Strike* was a modification of the video game *Half-Life* from the game developer Valve. At that time, eSports evolved into a competitive landscape, and many game developers did not understand what was happening (Asarch 2018). Blizzard Entertainment especially learned a significant lesson. It lost control of its game in South Korea, and a whole industry evolved without Blizzard Entertainment; subsequently, a profit was made from the audience, and it was not the game developer that benefitted. Out of that, a legal debate emerged that strengthened current understanding of the role of the game developer (Rogers 2012). Furthermore, many game developers realized their potential and, contrary to traditional sports, their unique role. In traditional sports, nobody owns football, for example; therefore, there is a process for making a product out of it. The game developer owns an eSports title, so there is an intellectual property and building a product out of it requires the legal and technical permission of the game developer (Partin 2018a). The game developer has an inherent power that grows over time.

Riot especially was a pioneer in game developing, creating content, tournaments, and leagues. Today, it is seeking to increase its power even further by creating franchises for its leagues in North America and Europe. Game developers are the natural gatekeepers, and many of the game developers understand their current role in the value network. Today, the majority of popular eSports titles are created by a small group of game developers, being Activision Blizzard, Tencent, and Valve. In the case of Activision Blizzard, Tencent owns a minority stake. The game developer owns everything surrounding the eSports title and can therefore control everything regarding the eSports title. However, making a great eSports title may not automatically qualify the game developer as a good tournament organizer. Activision Blizzard had to acquire the MLG to enhance its ability to create eSports content. Riot utilized the tournament organizer ESL to create the first event and started to do it on its own further along the road.

Being a natural gatekeeper may also be insufficient in some ways (Tushman and Katz 1980), but they are the rule-makers (Abanazir 2018). Although there is always the risk of competition and some other game developers creating a better or more desirable game, game developers can try to create a new version. Many cases highlight the risk of cannibalization. Concerning *Counter-Strike*, *Counter-Strike 1.6* competed for the same audience as *Counter-Strike Source*, and it needed another version, *Counter-Strike Go*, to reunite the audience under one banner. Another example is *StarCraft II*, which could not convince the South Korean audience, and therefore the development was so extreme that the *StarCraft* scene is a mere shadow of its former glory. The game developers are more involved than ever, and they try to harness their power as natural gatekeepers. Still, there is no one way to utilize their power, and there are various strategies for the game developer.

Consequently, there is a spectrum of strategies the game developer can choose (Fig. 3.2). These strategies can be categorized into ignoring, laissez-faire, the fate of the niche, regulating, and overregulating. Furthermore, several examples are depicted, and these eSports titles can be categorized as being essential titles in eSports. These strategies are currently predominant in the eSports industry, and many game developers are trying to establish their eSports title in alignment. However, this is under the existing premise that the game developer acts actively and willingly as the gatekeeper.

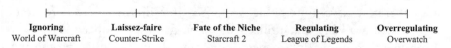

| Ignoring | Laissez-faire | Fate of the Niche | Regulating | Overregulating |
| World of Warcraft | Counter-Strike | Starcraft 2 | League of Legends | Overwatch |

Fig. 3.2 Spectrum of regulation strategies for the game developer

It may be counterintuitive to start with the ignoring strategy and *World of Warcraft* as an eSports title. Activision Blizzard tried to make *World of Warcraft* an eSports title with major tournaments in player versus player (PvP), and the game gained some audience, but, over time, *World of Warcraft* in terms of eSports became just a niche game with a small but loyal audience. With the release of the add-on legion, the game introduced the concept of the mythic dungeon running more broadly. Five players try to fight a dungeon within a particular time and with ever-increasing difficulty. Activision Blizzard was blind to this development for a long time and only recently introduced a tournament around this concept of player versus environment (PvE) as a media product that the audience may like. However, the game developer is just reacting in this game to the needs of the audience; therefore, the current success of *World of Warcraft* exists despite the work of Activision Blizzard. This ignoring strategy was particularly highlighted with the introduction of competitive raiding as something in which the audience can participate. The Method guild recently streamed mythic raiding live. Mythic raiding consists of 20 players battling the most difficult encounters: with the release of such content, there is a race for who will be the first to conquer these encounters. In the Uldir raid, the Method guild offered several streams from various players and peaked at over 250,000 viewers across all streams (McMillan 2018). This success will change the field of competitive raiding drastically, and many guilds will join this development; but, again, this is a development despite the efforts of the game developer. In the end, the ignoring strategy may be a way to outsource one's own ideas, but it also requires new content and new ideas from the game developer. The developers of *World of Warcraft* may ignore eSports, but the main focus lies on keeping the player in the game. Hypothetically, a stellar game developer could ignore the eSports aspect of its strategy, because its product is versatile enough to have an ever-shifting space in the game.

However, that may not be sufficient for many game developers, and they therefore try a more proactive approach. Still, the laissez-faire strategy is also available and utilized by some game developers. The most prominent example is *Counter-Strike* and how Valve is promoting *Counter-Strike*. This strategy does not mean that Valve is ignoring it, but it does not enforce too many regulations or have a rigid tournament schedule. The involvement of Valve exists, but it mostly supports the community surrounding the game. Everybody can create a tournament for *Counter-Strike* and Valve will, after meeting some requirements, support the tournament organizer.

Furthermore, Valve shows no interest in getting into franchising (Ashton 2018a). However, it performs its primary task and tries to balance *Counter-Strike* with patches, add new content, and so on. Interestingly, Valve is helping the community to have a variety of different tournaments by creating the Major Championship with a prize pool of $1,000,000 in 2018, but Valve is not organizing the event, and every major tournament organizer has the chance to be allowed to organize a Major Championship event. For example, in 2018 Faceit and ELEAGUE organized such an event, and in 2019 the ESL will host the next tournament in Katowice. As the term 'laissez-faire' implies, Valve is not ignoring the eSports potential of its game: it actively helps the game, but it is the invisible hand steering *Counter-Strike*. This strategy has led to robust self-organization on the *Counter-Strike* scene: tournament organizers try to minimize the cannibalization effects (this does not always work); players try to unionize themselves; and the audience has the chance to choose. The other Valve game, *Dota 2*, however, is more regulated, culminating in The International tournament, and consequently not entirely following the laissez-faire strategy. However, compared to other eSports titles, *Dota 2* is less regulated and "gleefully chaotic" (Zacny 2017). This shift in strategy may imply that the laissez-faire strategy requires a mature eSports title with a big and loyal audience. Still, the strategy to take a step back and let the market decide is, at least for Valve, a profitable approach.

The next strategy is called the fate of the niche strategy. It describes the situation wherein some eSports titles are just a niche game. However, that is nothing terrible where being a business is concerned—quite the opposite: game developers can create a balanced and sustainable business model out of this niche. Activision Blizzard is again an excellent example for this strategy. With their titles *Call of Duty*, *Heroes of the Storm*, *Hearthstone*, and *StarCraft II*, they became professionals in creating a niche league, but the cost-benefit ratio may not be hugely positive in some of these games. In *Heroes of the Storm* especially, Activision Blizzard tried desperately to escape the fate of the niche (Rizzo 2018). Interestingly, in *Hearthstone* they never tried to avoid the niche, and this makes the game successful, especially as it is fun to play and relaxing to view. The compelling case, however, is *StarCraft II*, especially as the game developer tried both to reconquer South Korea and transform *StarCraft II* into a global phenomenon. At the beginning, the eSports scene grew exponentially, and many tournaments around the world emerged. In his analysis of the development, Partin (2018b) explains that the move of Activision Blizzard to bring some regulation to the *StarCraft* scene may have led to the downfall of the competitive tournament scene, especially as the South Korean scene was dominating every tournament and the (Western) audience lost interest. From there on, every stakeholder was stuck in a downward spiral. That changed with the introduction of the region lock and trying to create a global scene rather than watching Koreans battle it out and hope for a miracle. Activision Blizzard actively sought to diversify its audience, and this can be observed in the move to make *StarCraft II* free to play. But, most importantly, it gave up becoming the pinnacle of eSports and accepted its fate in the niche, which makes the game a popular choice for many tournament organizers, as Michal Blicharz, vice president of programming at ESL, summarizes as follows: "StarCraft II works better at events where it's not alone. It's just a perfect blend of everything" (Blicharz, quoted in Partin 2018b). Being in the niche may not be a bad thing, especially looking at *Hearthstone* and *StarCraft II*: both games are cost-effective and have an existing audience that likes to watch those games. The niche may not lead to a big audience, but there is a sustainable audience. Still, the fate of the niche is something Activision Blizzard is not comfortable with, and in *StarCraft II*, the strategy to escape the niche nearly killed any interest in the game, while *Heroes of the Storm* is not attracting an audience compared to *LoL* and *Dota 2*. Activision Blizzard's newest game, *Overwatch*, may escape the niche momentarily. *Call of Duty* is a popular title in the US, but outside of it, there are not that many players, and the rumor that *Overwatch* teams were offered a franchise in the *Call of Duty* league is a signal that they want to escape the niche (Byers 2018). Escaping the niche seems to require substantial investment, and it is linked with a high risk of failure: any game developer trying to escape needs to gain momentum and keep this momentum up for a certain period to create a loyal audience. However, the fate of the niche could be a solid strategy for some game developers, as there is still much space in the niche, especially in an ever-growing market. This strategy can be undertaken in a cost-effective way and lead to a profitable and sometimes sustainable business model.

Other approaches toward the utilization of eSports titles are the regulating strategy and the overregulating strategy. Here, the game developer uses its power over the game and controls every part of the eSports scene. Besides creating new content and new updates, the game developers control what and how tournaments are played; they control how the players or teams are formed; and, most importantly, they have control over, or mostly self-organize, the major tournaments. A prominent example of such regulation is with *LoL*, for which the tournaments on the highest level around the world are organized by Riot, as is the production of the media content. In order to participate, the teams need to follow clear rules laid down by Riot. In recent years, Riot has transformed its leagues into franchise leagues, binding the teams even further to the league. Besides having sufficient capital and long-term sponsors, teams applying to become a franchise had to develop an extensive application manual, many details of which were shared with Riot. The goal is to control and steer the game and everything around the game the way they want it, and any stakeholder participating in *LoL* has to follow their rules. Still, it is questionable if the franchise gamble will lead to a higher degree of controllability and, as envisioned by Riot, to an increase in profitability. However, at least from a governance perspective, the increase in regulation grew naturally, and it seemed in regions like North America the next step to switch to a franchise-based league. Whether a franchise-based league will work in Europe is questionable, however (Volkov 2018), and 2019 will give some insights into this.

Still, *LoL* could be seen as being quite balanced concerning regulation, while the Overwatch League (OWL) is overregulated. The game developer Activision Blizzard is controlling every part of the professional environment in *Overwatch*. In contrast to *LoL*, the franchises in this league can apply and buy a distinct region, which they would own. This led to a situation in which the team London Spitfire was denied a meet and greet in Seoul by the Seoul Dynasty (Fitch 2018). Regulation that may seem reasonable, by adding a geolocational element into the mix, stifles the freedom and boundlessness of eSports. That may be a regulation that could be classified as minor, but other aspects are harmful to the eSports scene of *Overwatch*. The *Overwatch* system consists in tier 1 of the OWL, and in tier 2 of the regional Contenders league; however, no team in the Contenders league can be promoted to the OWL, thereby mimicking the concept of traditional franchise sports like baseball, basketball, and so on. Below the premier league, there are developmental and minor sports leagues or college teams that are supplying new talents. The goal of these leagues is to produce talents for the big leagues, and, in the case of *Overwatch*, this is the goal that Activision Blizzard envisioned. This goal may not co-align with the teams participating in the Contenders league. The game developer actively downgrades the second highest league in *Overwatch* to a farm league for the OWL teams, a situation that encourages Contender players to leave their team to become free agents and hope they will be picked up: if not, "there will be no trouble in finding a new Contenders team to join" (Carpenter 2018a). There is no incentive for any other organization to participate in this league and consequently, besides some academy teams, there are only temporary teams that may see it as some form of proving ground. However, recent downsizing measures will actually make the Contenders league irrelevant (Lewis 2018a).

Besides the recent downsizing in every region, the reaction of Activision Blizzard to the success of the Contenders league finals in China, having peaked at 1.25 million viewers (ESC.watch 2018a), was to add three new Chinese teams into the franchise. Consequently, this strategy highlights that the game developer is actively killing off any competition. This development may lead to more Chinese viewers for the OWL, but the Contenders league will become irrelevant. Riot, on the other hand, partially allows other leagues and tournaments around its leagues, while Activision Blizzard monopolizes all leagues in *Overwatch*: it controls them, and even the Overwatch World Cup, a nation's tournament, is tightly managed by Activision Blizzard. Trying to create a similar league system to football may sound promising, but it requires a specific structure below the actual professional league. There is an incentive to play in the NCAA, and there is also a chance to create a fan base in the NCAA. So, if Activision Blizzard copies the franchise system of North American leagues, there are two options available. Creating an NCAA league with universities could be helpful for the US, especially as there is an industry surrounding collegiate sports as well as an emerging interest from universities in eSports as varsity sports (Keiper et al. 2017), but that would mean a robust US-centric approach or making the Contenders league a minor franchise following the geolocational approach, diverging from the global league approach. However, this case shows that following the overregulation strategy also means dealing with every facet of the *Overwatch* scene.

One reason for the overregulation that may rival the overregulation of the Championship Gaming Series is the unknown risks Activision Blizzard is taking with this league, which can be observed in the following statement by the Overwatch League commissioner Nate Nanzer: "We didn't know what we didn't know before we launched the season" (Valentine 2018). It will be interesting to observe how it can manage the risk it is trying to minimize by controlling everything on its own. However, the track record of Activision Blizzard is not that great, as seen in the examples of *World of Warcraft* and *StarCraft*. Furthermore, it has already realized that it has to give the franchise teams some freedom and space to foster the team brand and a chance to foster local interaction (Fischer 2018).

Arcade or fighting games are missing, as there is no long-term dominance of one title. However, this sector in the eSports industry may be interesting for a different reason. The game developer may be the gatekeeper, but there is competition, and the tournament organizer can choose from a variety of potential eSports titles. Especially in the emerging game type Battle Royale, we observe a similar situation. Many game developers are creating such games and have to compete against other similar games. The gatekeeper logic only applies in an environment with little or no competition. There is no competition for *Counter-Strike* or *StarCraft*, and there is just a little competition between *League of Legends*, *Dota 2*, and *Heroes of the Storm*. However, in an environment with heavy competition, the role of the gatekeeper is dwindling, and the game developer has to fight for a spot in the eSports industry. That may describe the situation in Battle Royale, in which games like *Fortnite* and *PUBG* work actively with their scene, the tournament organizer, and the professional teams to find an exciting way to make an eSports title around their game.

For example, "Epic Games has remained nimble" (Miceli 2018a): it does not enforce its power, but works cooperatively with every stakeholder. This is similar to the game *PUBG* and many other emerging Battle Royale games. We may in the future observe more competition among eSports titles, and that may be a good thing, as the gatekeeper situation will be less relevant; however, it may explain why some game developers are trying to make a short-term profit and trying to bind professional teams through franchising to their leagues and forcing a few franchises to commit to the league. However, in the end, the audience can choose and will choose what eSports titles are relevant.

Tournament Organizer

In the current evolution phase of the eSports ecosystem, the game developers are the most important stakeholders, and they have the most power. Subsequently, at the moment, they have every legal right to monopolize every part of their game (Adomnica 2018). However, this behavior is still a rarity in eSports, and the emerging eSports titles often decide in favor of a cooperative strategy—for example, *PUBG* is cooperating with StarLadder (Kutateladze 2018) and OGN (Pei 2018) in creating its global league. Alternatively, the game *Rainbow Six*, which followed a slow and steady growth strategy, was supported in this development by the ESL to transform the game gradually into an eSports title. This development led to a league system similar to *LoL* (still with a relegation system), but in addition to this league, there will be various tournaments around the world (Murray 2018a). *Rainbow Six* is especially interesting from the perspective of the tournament organizers, as it shows a way to participate in this changing eSports environment. A strong move toward franchise leagues overshadowed 2018, predominantly because of *Overwatch* and *LoL*, while games like *Rainbow Six* has experienced a slow but organic growth over time. This growth can be attributed to the fact that tournament organizers shared their knowledge and the game developers listened. Although a peak viewership of 330,000 viewers may not sound that extraordinary, the numbers are gradually rising (ESC.watch 2018b) (this has yet to be verified). The tournament organizers have currently lost some power, as game developers like Activision Blizzard are pushing them out (Adomnica 2017). However, this may be a blessing in disguise, as tournament organizers have had to diversify their portfolio and look for new opportunities outside the major titles.

However, in the history of eSports, the tournament organizers have been a driving force, especially as the game developers often neglected their eSports title. The organizers filled the void actively and shaped the vibrant eSports scene of today. Especially in the beginning, it was essential to bring the competitors together to establish a fair competitive environment. At that time, the audiences were quite small, and a tournament had a somewhat intimate feeling. Nowadays, those tournaments often fill arenas (Thompson 2015). People want to participate in the tournaments "to be part of the gaming community, to watch their favorite players and teams, to connect with friends they played with and met online, to meet the pro players" (Eventbrite 2015, p. 3). The tournament operators saw the chance to evolve their business model around this changing environment. They can reach their audience on the live streams as well as the audience in the arena. People are traveling around the world to watch the teams compete, making them worthwhile events. At the same time, millions watch those tournaments via the live stream (Sjöblom and Hamari 2017).

Especially in times of increasing centralized league structures, tournament organizers add some variety to the eSports ecosystem. Tournaments can include various games, as well as tournaments in locations that are often neglected by the game developers. The underlying premise for the success of tournament organizers is that there is some form of competition in which the services of tournament organizers are required. However, this requires a healthy and competitive ecosystem. Interestingly, we can observe this in games like *Counter-Strike*, in which various tournament organizers (e.g., Blast, ELEAGUE, ESL, Faceit, PGL, StarSeries) compete for the best teams and the audience. As stated by Lampkin, "The general dream vision is that you have a market at all [...] levels, so when publishers want to work with a third-party organizer, there's a bunch of them" (quoted in Murray 2018b). Furthermore, creating an in-house league is expensive and requires many resources for a game developer; therefore, several game developers will require tournament organizers to have a working tournament structure, especially at the beginning. Even

Activision Blizzard needed to acquire the MLG (at that time, one of the most important tournament organizers in North America) to have the capability to create its league, while Riot started out working with tournament organizers like ESL to get its tournament operation running.

Consequently, tournament organizers have a distinct and vital role in the eSports ecosystem. They connect game developers with their respective audience and, furthermore, work on improving the interconnection between these two stakeholders. A reliable and professional tournament structure will also draw professional teams into the league. Picking up the example of *Rainbow Six*, a majority of the top eSports teams have a professional *Rainbow Six* squad. Therefore, the tournament organizers have specific capabilities, knowledge, and competencies that many game developers require for their eSports titles. In some cases, these tournament organizers also act as scouts for potential and promising games that could become eSports titles.

Furthermore, over the years many tournament organizers have become highly professional and highly efficient. As an illustration of how complex the preparation of a tournament is, the author talked with Chris Flato (Senior Communications Manager, ESL Global) about a rough generalization of the process of organizing a major tournament as every tournament has a unique environment and challenges to deal with. The tournament planning often starts around a year before the actual event. For some tournaments, like the events in Cologne (nicknamed 'the cathedral of *Counter-Strike*'), the ESL will have a feedback loop directly after the event. For events without a specific location, location scouting is essential. Such a location should have an enthusiastic crowd and should also have some support from the city; furthermore, it should be an exciting market for potential sponsors. It is crucial for the tournament organizer to have insight into the scope of the tournament: is it a major international event or a regional event? This decision also has an impact on the venue selection. Other aspects are an analysis of the games played in the region, as there are specific regional differences, and the time-slot: a tournament should ideally not collide with other major tournaments to minimize the cannibalization potential. All of those factors influence the selection of a location, but the ESL can create synergies for some of their stakeholders as well: for example, Mercedes showed some interest in the ESL One Genting event, predominantly as this was a way to foster their brand in Malaysia even further. After the location is selected, the preparation begins by finding the event sponsors and selecting the games, the venue, and the professional teams. The goal is to have most of the organizational aspects finalized to announce six months before the event. This announcement ideally includes the main sponsors of the event, as well as one or two top teams that will compete. After that initial announcement, over the next months the actual preparations start for the planning of the event. Stage planning for the venue, equipment transportation, and security planning are some essential aspects for making the event possible. In that time, the staff list evolves, along with what departments are necessary, whether the ESL has a regional headquarters that can support the event, and the people that will have to travel there. All of that has to be organized. At the same time, marketing is ongoing: new teams are announced continuously, promotions for the event are planned, and ticket sales begin. Preparations are necessary for the potential group stage. This group stage often takes place in a local hotel, but that also requires a specific infrastructure consisting of a playing area, a warm-up area, catering, and space for the press. For a major event, there is usually a core team of 20–30 people and up to 100 people from the ESL at the event. This number does not include the security, rigging teams, and caterers. Seven days (most often it is a Monday) before the event, the media material for the event is produced—pictures of the players, team presentation videos, and so on. Furthermore, the group stage begins. From Tuesday until Thursday, the group stage is played in the hotel, and on Wednesday the main stage is built. On Friday, the group stage is dismantled. Friday, Saturday, and Sunday are usually reserved for the main tournament. The whole time, the event leadership has to manage the marketing, public relations, player management, and so on. These days are the most exhausting, but the events are planned in every detail, and the ESL has become one of the most professional tournament organizers in the world. This professionalization can also be linked to the statement that some departments juggle ten events at the same time. An interesting side note Flato shared was that at the event in Cologne, the headquarters of the ESL was often empty as every employee was working or watching the event on site. He also said that the posters in the city were often not a way to get local people to watch the event, but rather so that the players could take selfies with them. These selfies are shared on social media, and these pictures are a great multiplicator to get more fans to the event or watching the event online.

This short case gives some insights into the complexity of creating an event, but also into the need for a tournament organizer to operate within a healthy ecosystem and a healthy business model network. The organizers have a crucial role of having tournaments with various game titles from various game developers. Such tournaments cannot be organized by the game developers, as they will focus only on their games. Furthermore, the tournament organizers have the chance to specialize on the creation of events and will be able to diversify the eSports environment. Only independent tournament organizers can have different titles in different tournaments in different locations. Furthermore, due to the competitive environment, tournament organizers have to adapt and innovate. Although the game developers are currently extremely powerful, the tournament organizers are keeping the variety of games up and actively seeking the next big title. Especially in this volatile market, eSports titles usually have a finite lifecycle, and it is still impossible to foresee the next big title, as seen with the surprising success of Battle Royale games. Tournament organizers have positioned themselves as enablers with a diversified portfolio. They are not one-trick ponies like the game developers. In the current evolution of eSports, this feature may sound like a disadvantage, especially as some game developers enforce their legal power quite drastically, but this is only because of a lack of competition (Adomnica 2017). However, eSports is not an industry with only a few games, but rather an industry with an ever-increasing number of titles (Besombes 2018). Consequently, the current diversification strategy and the ongoing search for new titles, new locations, and new partners may help them to create a sustainable business model in a volatile market, as they can proactively foresee changes and adapt to these changes quickly.

Professional Teams

Another relevant stakeholder in the eSports industry is the existence of professional teams. These teams are necessary to create a sustainable environment for competitions at the highest level. Similar to professional teams in traditional sports, these eSports teams try to get the best players possible and support them with coaches, training possibilities, and an environment in which they can focus solely on becoming better and beating the competition. To fund this support, revenues from sponsorship and prize money are shared to a certain degree. Players also get a certain salary, certain premiums, and, increasingly, health insurance and pension funds. In recent years, many of the professional teams have increased their professionalism massively, and they can compete with some traditional sports organizations. However, eSports has not yet solved the main problem that traditional sports share: what comes after retirement? Many teams try to help their players the best they can, by giving them access to a healthy diet or psychologists. Furthermore, they acquire funding and sponsorship to keep the business profitable and try to monetize the players through merchandise and other possibilities. The top organizations particularly are able to keep their best players for a long time and to identify and train new talents efficiently. Therefore, successful teams can balance short-term dynamics with long-term survivability; many of them have grown organically over time and have always tried to focus on the long-term profitability and, consequently, their business model.

Especially in this volatile market, there is high fluctuation in eSports teams, but, as depicted in Table 3.1, some teams created a brand for a long period of time. For example, the team SK Gaming was founded in 1997 and is still one of the most relevant organizations in eSports. Many of the teams in the list are so relevant that they can be classified as powerhouses in today's eSports industry. Nevertheless, the players have changed, and the titles the organizations are playing, the name of these teams, and the brand have become internationally known. The first generation of

Table 3.1 Examples of top teams in eSports divided according to founding time and region

	North America	Europe	South Korea	China
Up to 2000	Evil Geniuses	SK Gaming	KT Rolster	
2004–2005	CompLexity	Fnatic	SK Telecom T1	Team WE
2009–2011	Cloud9	Na'Vi	Jin Air Green Wings	Invictus Gaming
From 2015	Echo Fox	BIG	Gen.G	Royal Never Give Up

teams especially are beacons for the age of eSports, and there is a certain maturity involved in eSports. SK Gaming is over 20 years old, and this is a testament to the sustainability in a young, emerging, and volatile industry. Interestingly, the second generation of teams consists of some of the most successful organizations in eSports. Teams like Fnatic and SK Telecom T1 are synonymous with ongoing dominance. There are sometimes ups and downs, but in the big picture, they are mostly successful. The third generation highlights the establishment of teams surrounding the current growth cycle of eSports. In the shadow of the development of Twitch and *League of Legends*, a variety of teams was founded. Teams like Cloud9 already have a proven track record and can look back on various successes.

The latest generation since 2015 also points out a certain change in the eSports industry. More and more external stakeholders are involved in eSports. There are traditional sports organizations or players establishing professional teams (e.g., Echo Fox) and utilizing their name (e.g., FC Schalke 04), entrepreneurs (e.g., Gen.G), venture capitalist or investors (e.g., Immortals), or those founded by people from eSports (e.g., BIG). More and more teams are being bought by non-endemic stakeholders that want to invest in eSports, potentially out of fear of missing out or believing the existing hype. On the one hand, this development has led to a professionalization in the team organization; on the other hand, the focus on sustainability or long-term vision is getting vaguer. This becomes even more troublesome when some teams openly state that they are far from profitability (Cocke 2018a). In several talks with experts in the scene, a number pointed out that there is currently too much money and that some teams forget about their business model. If these external stakeholders start to demand a return on investment, this could lead to serious problems for some organizations. This development could already be happening for some organizations, as some of them have recently announced severe layoffs (e.g., Carpenter 2018b; Goldhaber 2018).

Still, there are many organizations with a strong focus on their business model and their profitability. For example, Fnatic always had a strong focus on becoming an independent organization without depending too much on external investors and, furthermore, reducing its dependence on sponsorship. Being a relatively old organization, it experienced the struggle of the financial crisis and had to adapt. It tries to harness the value of its brand and monetize its brand. It has a strong footing in merchandise and in 2015 introduced its hardware line of gaming peripherals called Fnatic Gear.

Still, the core business is to find and support players who will win tournaments. The interesting aspect of eSports is that it is possible to combine talents solely from a skills perspective. People can be chosen from all over the world. This freedom of choice leads to the importance of a support system surrounding the players. Training facilities are necessary, along with coaches, staff, analysts, balanced training routines, and a healthy diet. However, having the freedom to choose also leads to constant transfer shuffles. Although many leagues have transfer windows, these transfer times are sometimes extreme. In many teams, rosters are constantly changing, and it becomes necessary to be professional in forming teams.

Consequently, an essential question is whether talent is a sufficient criterion for selecting a team. As traditional sports already proved, a team needs to work together, to communicate, and to have a way to harmonize. In a globalized eSports world, culture could be an impacting factor.

As stated by Adler and Gundersen (2007), cultural diversity can have a positive impact on teams, under the assumption that creativity is required. Consequently, cultural diversity can have a beneficial influence in certain situations (Scholz 2012). Cultural diversity could be relevant for the composition in eSports teams, as creativity can lead to a competitive advantage. However, training is a routine task and essential for any successful eSports team. According to Adler and Gundersen (2007), cultural diversity is highly effective for the creative aspects of eSports, but also highly ineffective for the routine training of skills in eSports. Consequently, teams and coaches have to choose a specific path to select either a creative team or a team honing its skills.

Looking at the major tournaments in 2017 in the games *Counter-Strike*, *Dota 2*, and *League of Legends*, there is still a certain tendency to have teams from a single nation. This approach is often seen in teams from South Korea and China; however, there are also several teams consisting of a range of nationalities. The International in 2017 was won by Team Liquid, consisting of a South Korean coach and players from

Finland, Jordan, Bulgaria, Lebanon, and Germany. Interestingly, the data show that many teams in the top eight have a certain tendency toward either a highly individualistic and heterogeneous approach or a highly collectivistic and similar approach. It is unclear if the cultural approach was utilized knowingly or intuitively, but a certain tendency is observable. In the top eight of the three named games, eleven teams had an individualistic team composition, while six teams had a collectivistic team composition.

Consequently, looking at the cultural composition could or should be part of a team-building strategy. This highlights the potential of cultural optimization first and foremost in eSports. However, as eSports is highly volatile, it will be interesting to see if those patterns also evolve in the related context of accelerating business. In a highly global, highly digitized business context, the cultural dimensions of people still have an impact on team compositions. Moreover, even in business, since gamification is permeating it, the 'gamer culture' gains relevance (e.g., Cardador et al. 2017; Oprescu et al. 2014).

However, especially in the current and ongoing hype, more and more money is being invested in eSports and, most importantly, in professional teams. This money is flooding to create a situation in which some professional teams are neglecting the importance of a solid business model, focusing on creating a profitable business, or having sustainable growth. For example, there is an ongoing debate in *LoL* as to how many professional teams can make their business profitable. In 2017, H2K Gaming (Lippe and Tully 2017) and Unicorns of Love (Mallant 2017) raised the issue that the revenue sharing in *LoL* can be seen as a disadvantage for the teams, and H2K states that it operates with an annual loss of roughly $1 million. Especially in *LoL*, salaries have risen exponentially in recent years, leading to an environment in which players prefer yearly contracts as they can get a more lucrative deal next year. Moreover, several professional teams, in the wake of the transition toward franchises in many leagues, announced layoffs. At the same time, some teams are blindly charging into new endeavors to create short-term growth to please investors—for example, OpTic Gaming expanding to India. India may be a significant potential growth market, but it lacks a specific infrastructure, and there is still no particular audience. It is observable that there is a hefty increase in risks for professional teams in the current eSports environment. However, from a business perspective, the history shows that teams rarely survive taking uncontrollable risks. Many professional teams can get financing quickly at the moment, but having a business model combined with a distinct strategy and vision will, in the long run, offer a better chance of staying in the industry. Teams like KT Rolster, Fnatic, or Cloud9 will also have a pivotal role in eSports in the coming years, as they have the strategic agility to adapt proactively without taking too many risks.

Professional Players

Probably the most important stakeholder in the eSports industry is the professional player. At the same time, however, this stakeholder is sufficiently available in the market. Many amateurs do want to become professional players and make their money with gaming. Interestingly, it is even more challenging to break through than in other traditional sports, making it difficult to have a professional career in eSports and even more challenging to make enough money to live from a salary and prize money. Furthermore, players have to commit to a specific game so they have the chance to become masters. That specialization may be similar to traditional sports, but the lifecycle may be drastically shorter. So, on the one hand, playing video games competitively is predominantly possible at a young age, but on the other hand, video games on a competitive level do not have plannable longevity. This culmination explains the sharp focus of players to get as much money as possible in a short period, thereby sometimes being highly opportunistic. However, many teams, knowing that there is an abundance of talent, are also opportunistic. This leads to a highly competitive environment in which only the stars have enough power to negotiate with the professional teams.

This tense situation is observable in the inconsistency between salaries paid to players. For example, in the inaugural season of *Overwatch*, the majority of players had no star status and, consequently, the minimum salary was around $50,000 per year (Nanzer 2018), a little less than the average salary of $60,000 per year (JKCP 2018). However, the next season of *Overwatch* may change that drastically. Looking at *LoL*, players on average received a salary of $80,000 in Europe and $105,000 in North America (ESPN 2017), and in North America at least that has risen to around $320,000 on average per year in 2018 (Romain, quoted in Koueider 2018). Lee 'Faker' Sang-hyeok, considered the best player ever in *LoL*, is reportedly earning $2.5 million per year (Newell 2018). He may have even received offers of up to $4 million and based on the information provided by Hong 'YellOw' Jin-Ho the total earnings may be up to $4.6 million (Christou 2018). Faker was earning around $1.8 million through sponsorship and roughly $200,000 in prize money. However, this player is undoubtedly one of the most popular players in eSports. For many players, the prize money is an important source of income, and, according to esportsearnings.com, only 60 players had prize money going beyond $1 million, with the German *Dota 2* player Kuro 'KuroKy' Takhasomi currently topping the list at $4 million. Other games like *Counter-Strike* also have competitive salaries: the salary is usually around $200,000 for the top players in *Counter-Strike* (Komplett 2017).

Salary and prize money are essential for the players to gain income, but with contracts frequently being on a one-year basis and the increasing competition in tournaments, this becomes controllable and projectable. Some stability in players' earnings came through the emergence of streaming. Many players do try to get a steady revenue stream through streaming, leading to a situation in which players' income consists of up to 50% salary and sometimes sponsorship, up to 25% prize money, and up to 30% streaming revenues. Occasionally, players quit playing on a competitive level as they gain popularity through their streaming. For example, the player Brandon 'A_Seagull' Larned quit playing *Overwatch* for Dallas Fuel to return to streaming full time (D'Orazio 2018a). In some cases, this could be a less stressful way to make money without the training regimens and the competitive pressure. Streamers like Tyler 'Ninja' Blevins supposedly make around $500,000 per month (Booker 2018). This may be an extreme outlier, but a streamer with 2000 subscribers could make around $60,000 per year; compared to the $50,000 minimum salary in *Overwatch*, this could be a lucrative alternative.

Streaming may be especially lucrative for players with a loyal fan base compared to the harsh world of being a professional player. Several players highlight that they are getting tired, and some even quit because of burnout (D'Orazio 2018b). Comments like "I'm at my house all day, trying to get better" (Jablonowski, quoted in Campbell 2016) or "It's very hard to find a balance between a healthy amount of rest and optimal preparation, and it's a dilemma every team wrestle with" (Lasaitis, quoted in Carpenter 2018c) indicate burnout. Woodcock and Johnson (2018) raise an interesting aspect explaining the surge of players joining the eSports industry: "For many young people, the prospect of playing video games as a job is an exciting alternative to [...] work". Some research points in that direction, which has led to the concept of 'playbour' (Kücklich 2005). Playbour refers to players of video games blurring the difference between play and work (Castronova 2005) and it potentially becoming a craft (Brock and Fraser 2018). In a game, play transforms into work; it crosses from the playful context into the working context. This type of hybridization becomes evident in the field of competitive gaming, where players in eSports try to make a living out of a game (Taylor 2012). Work and play are blending, and this may become troublesome for professional players. Players have trouble relaxing, as everything is geared toward becoming a better player. For example, professional football players were often quoted at the World Cup in 2018 as playing *Fortnite* to relax (Alvarez 2018). In the *LoL* World Championship, some journalists are stating that playing *Fortnite* could have created a competitive advantage for team Cloud9 (Spiegel 2018). Being a professional player seems to be a realm in which work and life are entirely blurred, making it an extreme form of work-life blending.

The question of working conditions will be troublesome in the future and may be a way for any stakeholder in the eSports industry to gain a competitive advantage. In the current evolution of eSports, it may sound irrelevant as there is a steady stream of new talents, but without a motivating environment, keeping and binding the absolute stars to a specific team may be extremely difficult. It is observable that there are some improvements in training, health insurance, and pension funds (Lewis and Bradshaw 2017). For a long period in eSports, and especially in South Korea, the standard form of living for the players was in a training house with other team members and rarely any time for themselves. In recent years, the training facilities have become more professional and advanced (Jenny et al. 2018), and players often no longer live where the play happens, but have some work-life separation. Overall, professional eSports organizations try, increasingly, to take care of their players, especially as these players are the basis for any revenue stream for the professional teams and the product they sell to the audience. In times of short-term contracts, having players that identify with the team could lead to a way to ensure that the fans stay with the team.

Still, as stated before, eSports has the same challenge as traditional sports: there is only a short time frame in which players can compete at the highest level. There are alternative careers later on as coaches, analysts, coordinators, hosts, and broadcasters, but not every player is capable of taking on one of these roles, and sometimes it is a matter of luck to find a job in eSports afterward. Furthermore, players often start at an early age and neglect their education, making the situation even grimmer. The professional player's career has to pay off or it could be seen as a waste of time. Some teams give the players a chance of vocational training or enable them to study, but the majority often have no alternative career plan. Introducing a collegiate sports environment was a concept that may have worked for traditional sports; however, in eSports, players often peak in their early 20s; they are therefore missing out on the opportunity. Consequently, players need to think about their future, and it may be a solid choice to return to university after their professional career. This could allow the chance for an education and improve the emerging collegiate eSports scene without the fear that talented players will drop out and join a professional team.

Providers and Communities

Game developers, tournament organizers, professional teams, and professional players can be categorized as primary activities following Porter's value chain (1985). However, to create a product for the audience, several support activities are necessary. These support activities are essential to reach a broader audience and to increase the potential monetization of the audience. There are infrastructure providers, service providers, hardware providers, and community enablers.

Firstly, the infrastructure providers are essential for reaching the audience wherever and whenever they want to consume eSports content.

Twitch in particular contributed greatly to that area with an easy way to follow the matches, as it was challenging to follow the tournaments in the early 2000s. Today, everybody can stream their matches and everybody, potentially, can watch these games. For a long time, Twitch was the only provider of such a service, but today there is Azubu, Facebook, YouTube, and many other smaller streaming platforms. This is beneficial for the audience, as there is an ongoing competition to improve the viewing experience. There are various ways to keep the audience hooked, not only by having coverage of great games, and viewers are incentivized to follow the games. For example, in *Overwatch*, viewers can get in-game skins of their favorite teams by watching the games. Besides the online audience, the offline audience requires a specific infrastructure. Equipment has to be carried around the world and stages have to be built. The ESL benefitted heavily from being acquired by MTG, as it now has access to a variety of providers that help it to transfer necessary equipment more efficiently. Furthermore, dedicated training facilities or eSports cafés are built in various locations, as well as a dedicated arena for eSports. This development may create a comprehensive infrastructure for any eSports-related topics and may foster local and regional communities even further.

Secondly, the service providers enrich the eSports environment through necessary services. One crucial aspect is the journalistic coverage of the eSports scene. Platforms like Dot Esports or ESPN Esports have improved drastically, creating an environment which may be comparable to traditional sports journalism. The coverage includes investigative reports as well as insight information on transfer rumors. However, it is not only the sports aspect that is covered by these service providers: for example, the Esports Observer contributes information on the business perspective. Several consulting agencies are emerging, as well as companies focusing on market research. Other companies try to supply the market with game analytics.

Additionally, law agencies focus on eSports-related law topics and talent agencies represent individual players. Another sector for service providers is the betting and gambling potential in eSports. The betting topic is an ongoing debate in both traditional sports and eSports, and eSports has had its share of scandals surrounding match-fixing, such as the arrest of 12 *StarCraft* players in 2015 (Sinclair 2015) or the scandal in North

America between the teams of iBUYPOWER and NetcodeGuides.com (Chalk 2015). However, it seems that the eSports industry is as prepared in relation to the topic of match-fixing topic as traditional sports (ESIC 2016). Anyhow, the rise of eSports betting companies as a service provider can be a helpful way to improve the audience's viewing experience.

Furthermore, betting companies like Betway and Unikrn have established long-term sponsorships with eSports teams. In the case of Betway, this sponsorship deal is for over three years, not a common scenario in eSports (Berc 2018). The eSports context also allows betting companies to go beyond just cash bets or fantasy sports, extending to bet skins or virtual items within a game (Hippeau 2018). Ultimately, these service providers help to foster the growth of eSports by giving additional value for the audience. There may be legal and regulatory obstacles, but even those challenges help the eSports ecosystem to grow. At the same time, it is also beneficial for the betting industry, as the eSports environment allows the testing of innovative and novel ideas to enhance the betting experience of the digital audience (Macey and Hamari 2018).

For the eSports industry, the hardware providers are essential as they benefit most from a thriving eSports industry and they have a keen interest in reaching the audience to monetize them. Like any other branch of sports, eSports requires specialized equipment (e.g., keyboard, mouse, headset, mousepad). Companies like SteelSeries, HyperX, and Razer were established to respond to this need and are both popular and highly profitable today. Logitech and Intel have long been part of the eSports scene and have had dedicated eSports departments for over ten years. In Q1 of 2018, Logitech reported a 60% growth in gaming products (Gurdus 2018). There are striking similarities to sports companies like Nike: companies like Logitech creating keyboards, and getting a team or a player to use their products, will potentially lead to an increase in sales. Consequently, it has to invest in those teams and players. Furthermore, these companies have to carry out research and development to create better equipment and better tools for the players to improve their performance and, subsequently, create new products for the audience to buy.

Finally, the community enablers are essential to bring the audience together and foster interaction. These enablers go beyond the other stakeholders in bringing the people together and, most importantly, are often self-organized. There is a robust communal aspect to attending an eSports event in an arena, but it is not always possible to watch the events in such an arena, especially as the major tournaments are staged all around the world. Consequently, the audience organizes or attends so-called viewing parties. This phenomenon became popular with *StarCraft* and their BarCraft. BarCrafts often take place in a local bar, where the audience watches a game and has a great time. This concept was the basis for a thriving business model of dedicated eSports bars, the most prominent being the franchise of Meltdown, which currently has over 60 bars in France, Germany, Canada, and other countries.

In summary, the supporting stakeholders enrich the variety of eSports as well as enable the potential to reach the dedicated audience. These stakeholders help to keep the audience involved and create an exciting and joyful experience. Still, without interacting with the other stakeholders, they do not have the basis for a healthy business model: for example, eSports journalists require events and players to discuss, and dedicated eSports facilities have similar needs. Streaming platforms need someone to produce content, and hardware providers utilize the eSports competition to sell their products. Still, not every supporting stakeholder depends entirely on eSports to thrive; for example, eSports is important for Twitch, but much of its content is created outside of eSports. The stakeholders understand the importance of eSports, and being part of the growth can be beneficial in the long run.

Secondary Stakeholders

Governing Bodies

A significant aspect of criticism of eSports is the seeming lack of governance (e.g., Hollist 2016; Chao 2017; Holden et al. 2017a, b). This argument co-aligns with the claim that eSports are like the Wild West. However, there are various entities in eSports that do try to create a specific governance, but it is important to highlight that eSports is just an umbrella term for various games. Traditional sports federations like the Olympic Committee demand that eSports have a governing organization that enforces the rules and regulations of the Olympic movement (Reuters 2018). The underlying message is that eSports should adopt the structures and regulations of traditional sports, and that could be a valid proposition, but eSports may not fit with these structures (Blicharz, cited in Miceli 2018b). Furthermore, talking about the entirety of eSports is presumptuous from a governance perspective. This envisioned top-down governance structure would mean not only uniting all stakeholders in one combined federation but also compelling all future eSports titles and all emerging eSports nations to join this global federation.

Interestingly, the equivalent of a global and overarching governance structure in sports would be the Global Association of International Sports Federations (GAISF), which does not include all sports played around the world. Furthermore, the mission of the GAISF is not to govern every federation in the world, but to bring federations and stakeholders together (GAISF n.d.). Consequently, traditional sports and several other institutions demand an introduction of governance structures for all eSports, something they fail to create for traditional sports.

Many secondary stakeholders do not realize that eSports describes a range of different games, different stakeholders, and, actually, everybody playing video games competitively. Consequently, eSports is ungovernable by one clear authority. There are several approaches to achieving governance more traditionally through federations, but they lack legitimacy in the eSports scene. There is an equivalent to an international governance body called the International e-Sports Federation, consisting of various national federations all over the world; on the other hand, there are industry-driven governance structures like the World Esports Association (WESA), founded by major industry brands. Beyond those attempts, the game developers own the game and have every legal right to change the game in any way they want. It becomes evident that creating governance structures mimicking those of traditional sports may not be sufficient, particularly as young sports also do not follow those suffocating structures. For example, the World Skateboarding Federation tries to be the umbrella organization for all types of skateboarding and its mission is to grow and connect involved stakeholders, promoting the sport: the only aspect of regulation is about creating a centralized scoring system (WSF n.d.). Compared to governance structures like the NBA or the NFL, it is even more striking that the business focus increasingly overweighs the sport interests (Ejiochi 2014). For example, the NBA team New York Knicks is the most valuable team, although it rarely succeeds in the playoffs (Forbes 2018). Everybody talks about the need for governance, but everybody understands something completely different by it. Something that fulfills every role is impossible to achieve.

Therefore, it is essential to consider the term 'governance' in more depth. There seems to be a unilateral understanding, at least in eSports, that governance means some entity having the power and legitimacy to decide the norms and regulations of eSports. UNESCO defines governance as follows: "In a broad sense, governance is about the culture and institutional environment in which citizens and stakeholders interact among themselves and participate in public affairs. It is more than the organs of the government" (n.d.). In research, governance is often seen as a process of organization and coordination without dictating norms and regulations (Bevir 2012). In this definition, the misconception in the discourse about eSports becomes evident. Governance in eSports is not a way to create a top-down structure of regulations, but rather the emergence of a bottom-up consensus of necessary social norms. Any stakeholder has to follow the rules and regulations created outside the eSports industry by, for example, the respective government and the law. However, the federation approach envisioned by the Olympic Committee will be impossible to achieve as there is nobody powerful enough to enforce such regulations.

This type of governance mimicking sports could also be harmful, as the eSports industry would bow to the traditional sports governance model. However, without a particular hierarchy, governance in eSports would focus on the coordination and organization of all stakeholders efficiently and transparently. This stakeholder-driven approach can be found in corporate governance (Lin 2011), and the focus lies on creating an environment that allows a thriving environment for the eSports industry. This could be the basis for a governance approach for the eSports industry, as corporate governance focuses on the rights and interests of all stakeholders, shares the responsibilities, ensures integrity and ethical behavior, and enforces transparency (OECD 2004). It additionally means that, in a volatile industry, governance principles are emerging bottom-up and could change over time. Still, there are already several unwritten principles in eSports that influence the way governance is done.

There are several examples of self-organized governance in eSports that emerged over time. The Counter-Strike Professional Players Association (CSPPA) is a union created by the players for the players, focusing on improving the working conditions and giving players a unified voice (Rohan 2018). This union was a reaction to the struggle *Counter-Strike* had in 2016 when players were exhausted by their "brutal schedule" (Campbell 2016). Another example is the Esports Integrity Coalition (ESIC), founded after incidents concerning doping and match-fixing. With other stakeholders in the industry, it spearheaded the development of specific vital structures and regulations, as well as a code of ethics and code of conduct (ESIC 2016), filling a void that was becoming harmful for every eSports stakeholder. Necessary solutions and governance principles emerge when a problem becomes apparent.

Furthermore, the necessary legitimation in eSports concerning self-governance could come from the various stakeholders themselves. Especially in Germany, there is an ongoing debate about whether eSports is a sport. This debate is symptomatic of the situation of eSports, and many traditional sports organizations fight against eSports. However, this fight may become less relevant as sport goes gray (Lombardo and Broughton 2017) and, especially, as stakeholders may decide independently what is the best strategy. In 2018, McDonald's Germany did not renew its 15-year partnership with the German Football Association in favor of increasing its sponsorship of eSports, mainly due to the reach toward a young audience (Ashton 2018b). Companies like McDonald's, Mastercard, Mercedes-Benz, or DHL show that they are committed to the eSports industry and that legitimizes its self-governance. Furthermore, an increase in eSports titles will lead to a decrease in the power of the game developer as well as motivate other game developers to create eSports titles. The recent hype around Battle Royale led to various games with an eSports tournament landscape, most predominantly *Fortnite* and *PUBG*. Both game developers, in cooperation with tournament organizers and the community, are trying to find the right way to create a tournament landscape for their game. At the same time, existing games like *League of Legends* and *Counter-Strike* strive to enhance their longevity.

Also, many other stakeholders are joining the eSports industry, adding to the fragmentation. In general, the eSports industry will become more diverse, increasing the competition. However, this highlights the importance of a sustainable business model within the business model network of eSports. The eSports industry may be growing more fragmented, but the general principles of coopetition, co-destiny, and convergence will be more essential for the growth of the business model. Especially with the looming crisis, the focus will be on the business model, and that is a valuable lesson to learn. Surviving in the eSports industry is based on strategic management and the realization that creating a business will require the support of the various stakeholders in the eSports industry. In the future, there may be fragmentation, and that may lead not only to a business model network for a distinct eSports title but also to a meta-business model network for the holistic eSports industry.

In general, the ongoing creation of governing bodies and governance is a typical phenomenon for emerging industries; however, many different embodiments are making it difficult to find the right governance solution. It is difficult to define what eSports is; therefore, it is difficult to find the right method of governance. Consequently, bottom-up corporate governance, with all stakeholders working together, may be a meaningful approach.

Sports Organizations

The tendency to link eSports with sports is pervasive (Adamus 2012; Hebbel-Seeger 2012) and has sparked intensive discussions about the appropriateness of doing so (e.g., Jonasson and Thiborg 2010; Witkowski 2010; Taylor 2012; Franke 2015; Hutchins 2008; Jenny et al. 2017). More and more researchers are focusing on the question of whether eSports is a sport (e.g., Holden et al. 2017a, b; Rosell Llorens 2017; Cunningham et al. 2018; Hallmann and Giel 2018; Parry 2018), and there is also a rift in the eSports scene concerning this topic: "to think that a new phenomenon like eSports can be described in terms of the old is to misunderstand it entirely" (SuperData 2015, p. 3).

It is a debatable topic, but it is undeniable that more and more sports businesses are investing heavily in eSports. Recent years especially have seen a massive spike in sports businesses establishing a foothold in the eSports industry. Interestingly, the narrative is rarely about sports, but is purely business-driven. Many sports businesses struggle to gain an international audience, and lesser known teams can no longer compete against the big names like FC Barcelona or Manchester United. There are not that many fields remaining in which there is still growth potential and a global market: in recent research, these 'star' markets are the FIFA World Cup, the English Premier League, and the NBA (Roberts 2018).

Furthermore, the sports audience is going gray. Lombardo and Broughton (2017) found that its average age is increasing. For example, the NBA had an average of 42 years in 2016, up from 40 in 2006, and the NFL average age increased from 46 years in 2006 to 50 years in 2016. Even football is moving toward an average age of 40 years. Many professional sports businesses have a problem reaching a young audience. The eSports industry is a global market with massive growth potential and reaches a younger audience.

Achieving growth in the main sports business is becoming increasingly difficult and may lead to increased risks for the business model; therefore, there is an ongoing strategic approach to diversify sports businesses. Schmidt and Holzmayer (2018a) developed a framework based on regionality and business proximity, categorizing the activities of sports businesses. For example, the NFL has one game in London to reach a global audience, but is sticking to its core business. Another example is the basketball division of FC Bayern Munich, focusing on a national market, but a sport generally unrelated to football. The eSports industry has become a different environment in which many sports businesses are trying to diversify their businesses.

In 2018, there are more than 200 sports teams with some form of eSports team in their organization. Up to 2015, there were fewer than ten sports organizations with involvement in eSports and the numbers are exponentially increasing. However, there are various types of strategic action concerning eSports:

1. Individual players for the digital version of the core business.
2. eSports teams for a variety of games.
3. eSports teams for a variety of games in a different country.

4. Joint ventures with an existing eSports team and creating a new brand.
5. Temporarily withdrawing from eSports.
6. Creating a dedicated league.
7. Buying a franchise team.

Type 1 describes the typical approach of many European football teams, as it has become customary to have some FIFA players or PES players wearing the team strip. The goal is to bind new players to the professional team, especially as this approach tackles the core businesses of any sports team and could potentially lead to new fans (van der Sar 2016).

Type 2 is less common, as it incorporates a high commitment of the sports business to a specific game that is unrelated to the actual brand. The primary challenge is that the actual brand is linked. The most prominent example is FC Schalke 04, which has a *League of Legends* team: it remains committed to this decision and even highlights that it wants to introduce eSports to its football fans (Schmidt and Holzmayer 2018b). The utilization of their brand led to new ways to reach a different audience, and the Schalke brand will be strengthened for the young, global, and digital audience (Schilling 2016). In the 2018 season of *LoL*, FC Schalke 04 nearly went to the World Championships, leading to the following comment from Tim Reichert (head of the eSports department): "From a business point of view, if we go to Worlds this would mean so much to the club. It would be massive to have a global audience, global eyeballs everywhere with millions of people" (Reichert, quoted in Elsam 2018). However, this type of strategic action is often used by lesser known sports businesses as a way to attract an international audience.

Type 3 is a rarity but, from a business perspective, it is understandable to create an eSports team in a different country, utilizing the brand to make it accessible. For example, in March 2017 Olympique Lyon signed a Chinese eSports team to be part of its internationalization strategy. This move was perceived as "a fascinating move by Lyon and a logical attempt at growing its brand overseas and reaching a whole new fan base" (Cooke 2017). Especially for an organization like Lyon, this could be a way to generate a fan base in direct competition to Manchester United and other already big names in China.

Type 4 is utilizing the existing capabilities and competencies in eSports to form a partnership or even a joint venture. This could lead to the establishment of a new brand, as done by FC Copenhagen with the *Counter-Strike* team called North, or a partnership created by Paris Saint-Germain FC and the *Dota 2* team LGD Gaming. Both sports businesses had less risk as they utilized established organizational structures, enabling them to have a strong standing in the eSports scene. North especially is seen as one of the powerhouses in the Nordic countries, and LGD Gaming just finished second in The International in 2018. This form of partnership is helping those sports businesses to get a foothold without creating any structures on their own. It may be a way to grow into the eSports industry naturally.

Type 5 is unusual, as the partnership of PSG and LGD was not the first attempt in eSports. PSG had a *LoL* team like FC Schalke 04, but withdrew from the league in October 2017 because the league seemed to be overheating: "Our Challengers Series experiences lead us to wonder about the League of Legends competitive scene economic balance" (PSG 2017). However, such a withdrawal is not common, and PSG was only partially withdrawing. Still, the first sports organization in eSports is no longer part of the scene. The German organization SSV Lehnitz joined eSports in 2002 and left in 2006. At one time, it even had an entirely Swedish team for *Counter-Strike*.

Type 6 is an approach that is becoming more common as more and more league operators try to create a digital structure for their traditional sports. For example, one of the first eSports football leagues, E-Divisie, was launched in the Netherlands in January 2017 with the following aim: "We see the E-Divisie as an extension to the existing range of football we offer, in which we can focus even more on young people. For the clubs, it is a fantastic platform for increasing the fans' involvement and jointly generating new content" (Tielbeke 2017). Many leagues followed that example, and the NBA 2K League, for example, will have a strong commitment from the NBA.

Type 7 is a more recent development, as leagues for *LoL* and *Overwatch* started to franchise in 2018. Any organization is locked into the league, and it may lead to long-term plannability for sports businesses. The North American scene especially is favoring the franchise model, and it is a simple way for any stakeholder to buy into the highest competitive league. For roughly $10 million it was possible to get a slot in the highest North American *LoL* league, and a slot for the inaugural season of *Overwatch* was worth around $20 million (Wolf 2017). The franchise model works especially well in the US, as the sports businesses see the similarities. There are seemingly enough observable parallels with existing franchise leagues that it was possible to sell the product (Youngmisuk and Wolf 2018). In *Overwatch*, for example, the Kraft Group owning the New England Patriots acquired the Boston Uprising, and the Comcast Group owning the Philadelphia Flyers got the Philadelphia Fusion. In *LoL*, Golden State Warriors invested in the Golden Guardians, and Clutch Gaming is backed by the Houston Rockets (Massaad 2017). At least for *Overwatch* and *LoL*, there is some observable convergence toward the North American approach to professional sports (Webster 2018).

There are many ways to approach eSports from a sports business per-spective. Expanding to eSports is a strategic decision. The question about the utilization of the brand is essential. There are challenges to being FC Schalke 04, PSG.LGD, Golden Guardians, or North that may also influ-ence the core business. Furthermore, the Golden Guardians coming last in 2018 shows that a successful sports organization may not translate auto-matically into a successful eSports organization. Being part of a franchise will help many sports organizations to survive the struggle of the first years, but they have to adopt the rules of the eSports scene to compete. A differ-ent approach is to find an operations partner, something the new Vancouver franchise in *Overwatch* has recently done by naming Luminosity (Murray 2018c). Still, with its audience going gray, sports businesses have to look for alternative approaches to reach the global, young, and digital audience, especially where the competition is already fierce. Sports businesses are competing against eSports organizations, investors, and corporations.

Sponsors

A driving force in eSports for an extended period was, and still is, spon-sorship. Based on a report by PwC (2018), a third of the eSports econ-omy can be contributed to sponsorship. Other reports, such as that from

SuperData (2018), show that nearly 60% of the revenues derive from sponsorships and advertising. Although industry reports always come with a specific caveat, in the eSports context especially, as there is rarely a chance to verify the data, it is essential to highlight that many eSports business models depend on some form of sponsorship, a situation that has been common in eSports for a long time.

In the beginning especially, many eSports businesses did not have alternatives to monetize their products and businesses. Merchandise was uncommon, and many organizations did not have the metrics to share with potential sponsors. It was nearly impossible to answer a question concerning returns on investment in eSports. Consequently, endemic companies were the main sponsors, as they understood eSports (Lake, cited in Nordmark 2018). Until today, those endemic companies like Intel, Logitech, or Nvidia have been the most loyal and committed sponsors in eSports. Other relevant sponsors are energy drinks like Red Bull or Monster Energy, labels that are seen as the best known sponsors in eSports (Sponsors 2018).

In recent years, it is observable that more and more non-endemic sponsors are joining the eSports scene. Companies like Mercedes-Benz recently expanded their support for the ESL until 2020 (Jordan 2018). Deloitte is sponsoring the ESL Dutch Championship (Deloitte 2018), and Mastercard is becoming the global partner for the *LoL* World Championship (Mastercard 2018). Other interesting examples are the DHL or Wüstenrot. The narrative is often comparable to the following statement from Mercedes-Benz: "As a global brand, we want to open ourselves up to new target groups. Esports gets us into a dialogue with young people, especially those with an affinity to technology" (Seeger 2018). Participating in eSports as a sponsor can help to get the brand to audiences that are difficult to reach via traditional methods. In particular, a young audience and an international audience can be achieved through sponsoring cost-effectively. Even companies like Nike were quite hesitant, but recently signed the Chinese superstar Jian 'Uzi' Zihao (Carp 2018), enabling them to improve their brand awareness in China.

There is a lot of space for any brand to be part of eSports, and there is an increase in insurance companies looking to sponsor. This development highlights that even though eSports has a mainly young audience, they have healthy lives, and they need insurance. However, it may not be sufficient to give some money for advertising. The study of Sponsors (2018) concerning brand awareness showed that companies like Logitech had succeeded in becoming recognizable. However, Sennheiser, a long-time sponsor of eSports, was often ignored by the audience. Although they sponsored SK Gaming back in the early 2000s and recently started supporting the University eSports league in Germany, they are not seen as authentic and therefore fail to monetize from their sponsorship.

Creating authenticity may be difficult for different corporations, but there are some aspects to consider: feed the passion, be willing to take some hits, speak the language, and give up control (Schultz 2017). These aspects highlight the skeptical view of non-endemic sponsors in eSports, and the sponsors have to prove their sincere interest by keeping in the loop. Furthermore, several non-endemic brands were successful because they were open to help and even gave up some of their power. The eSports audience is unique, and getting help from the primary stakeholders is an efficient way both to create an authentic partnership and to learn to understand this audience. There is still space for innovations in eSports, and sponsors can utilize the branding opportunities for a young and global audience, but being authentic is the key to success (Mitchell 2018).

General Public

Another essential secondary stakeholder is the general public, as they influence the general perception of eSports and, subsequently, the business related to eSports. The growth of eSports is still hindered by the perception that video games are bad for people, with the argument that video games make people aggressive, and this aggression may lead to shootings, endangering the general public; alternatively, video games are addictive, and addicted players will lose any control over their life. Although there are studies that show video games could have a beneficial effect, such as on hand-eye coordination, there is an absolute divide in the general public. Especially concerning eSports, this struggle makes it challenging to create a profitable business model. Interestingly, dealing with this topic highlights the need for eSports to exercise corporate social responsibility to change the perception of the general public. Tackling this problem is necessary to minimize this source of risk, as condemning video games or eSports is more comfortable for the general public than solving the actual reasons.

However, this is not the only factor about which the general public may be critical concerning eSports. Although women make up half of the video gaming population, they are incredibly underrepresented in the professional eSports scene, predominantly in professional players. From a biological perspective, there is no difference; but, with a handful of exceptions, women are not part of the professional player scene. There is an ongoing discourse about the reasons for that, and the AnyKey organization is fighting against the stereotype, but it is wrong to waive the diversity topic entirely. Research shows that mixed gender teams have a positive effect on performance (Apesteguia et al. 2012). It is interesting to observe that the research done on cultural diversity and its positive effect on creativity (Adler and Gundersen 2007) is utilized in eSports: various teams comprising different cultures beyond any language barrier are successful. Still, mixed gender teams in eSports are non-existent, although research in the business context shows a potential increase in performance for such teams. With the acquisition of Se-yeon 'Geguri' Kim for the Shanghai Dragons, there is the chance for the first time to observe a mixed gender team in action.

Investors, Entrepreneurs, Media, and Shareholders

Finally, various stakeholders have an impact on the eSports scene, but less due to a desire to change, shape, or influence eSports: the main focus lies on making a profit from eSports. This is especially the case for investors, entrepreneurs, and shareholders. The media are included here as they learned from their previous endeavors in eSports and, rather than changing eSports, they mostly adapt to the eSports scene. However, a profit-focused strategy can also be dangerous for an eSports organization dealing with such stakeholders.

In just the first half of 2018, over $700 million were invested in eSports companies, and those are just the disclosed investments (Azevedo 2018). Companies like Tencent are quite active in that field, trying to increase their power in the eSports industry. At the moment, money is flooding into eSports, and there will come a time in the future when these investors will demand a return on investment. Still, the flood of money has led to an environment in which valuations are inflated and highly speculative, costs are higher than they should be, and many believe that eSports will be the next big thing (Li 2018). All of these developments have led to rumors about a new bubble in eSports, and recent layoffs may fuel this rumor further (Cocke 2018b). Some are even stating that we may see a revival of the bubble created in the midst of the CGS, "so now we're here again. Venture Capital groups falling over themselves to invest in anything and everything esports. The word 'esports' is forced into things that would be ignored otherwise. Sports stars and celebrities want the joy of being a franchise owner without the billions needed to do it in the mainstream sports world. I am told daily that this time it is real, that we are now legitimately too big to fail" (Lewis 2018b). Consequently, there may be a risk that investors and entrepreneurs will demand results and want to see the significant growth rates everybody is dreaming of. The demand for growth may lead to risky endeavors that, without solid strategic planning, could lead to uncontrollable danger (Smith 2018). Another example is the struggle of Amazon to make Twitch an efficient and profitable product (Kain 2018).

Interestingly, the media businesses involved in eSports seem to have learned their lesson and understand eSports as a way to digitize their industry (Scholz and Stein 2017). MTG acquired the ESL and DreamHack, but they do not interfere with the business: they are trying to create professional structures in the organization and are focusing on helping on the operational level. MTG increased its ownership even further (MTG 2018) and showed its trust in the company, Turtle Entertainment. TBS, the media company behind the ELEAGUE, also seems to understand the eSports industry and does not force the league to produce for traditional media; instead, it utilizes the traditional media to get new audiences for its Twitch content (Taylor 2018). Media companies like the German ProSiebenSat.1 Sports approach the topic of eSports from a different angle: rather than replacing live streaming, they are trying to act as a bridge between the experienced eSports player and the occasional viewer, as well as creating a time-constrained show for tournament highlights (Ashton 2018c). This is a cooperative approach, as eSports can learn from traditional media and traditional media from eSports.

A more difficult stakeholder is the actual shareholder, as they are often unknown, and they are demanding a rising share and an increasing quarterly figure. However, eSports are often an investment in the future, so it may be difficult to give the shareholder the numbers they want, a development that is observable at Activision Blizzard and Tencent. Activision Blizzard collected high buy-ins for its franchises (ranging from $20 to $60 million), as well as a two-year media licensing deal with Twitch for $90 million (Baccellieri 2018). This helped to increase the shareholder value in the short term, but it will be interesting to observe what happens in two years. A similar situation can be observed with Tencent and Riot. Tencent owns Riot, and it is rumored that Tencent was worried about the decline in profits (Mickunas 2018): that may have led to the move toward franchises, to have a steady revenue model to reverse the decline in profits.

Audience as a Shared Target for Value Creation

The core of all stakeholders is the audience, and every stakeholder wants to monetize the audience. However, the audience is also actively participating in the eSports industry. The eSports audience is aligned with the gaming culture (Jonasson and Thiborg 2010; Franke 2015) or gamer culture (Shaw 2010). The eSports audience share a "self-professed passion for video games" (Weststar 2015, p. 1244). Consequently, there are no distinct boundaries in the eSports industry, and being the audience could also mean being a member of a professional team. There is a dynamic and ongoing transition between being the audience and creating content for the audience (Taylor 2012). There are no distinct boundaries: all stakeholders are part of eSports and are distinctly linked to one another. This integration process appears much more intense than is seen in any other cultural or sports-related phenomenon. "Altogether, professional gamers, audience members, and commentators present a dynamic understanding [of] video games as a performative medium" (Randhawa 2015, p. 16).

There is an inherent interdependence between the stakeholders and the audience: "We need casuals playing games we [the hardcore players] don't necessarily care about so that they can watch us now and then and enjoy themselves" (Schenkhuizen 2013, p. 31).

Consequently, all stakeholders depend on each other to foster the eSports industry further, and even the audience follows the fundamental characteristics: "[T]hey devote hours upon hours to mastering it, endlessly fascinated by the intricacies of the system, its characters, its weapons, its properties" (Taylor 2012, p. 89). This is important when trying to understand the dynamics of the interactions among the various actors in the eSports industry, as well as their potential for cooperating, even with competitors. This interconnection of the audience is also relevant for the secondary stakeholders that joined the eSports industry recently, primarily as they focus on short-term profits. Short-term gain is possible, but it could lead to long-term failure; therefore, a sustainable business model requires the integration of the audience as an integral part of this business model. The audience is the producer as well as the buyer of the product.

References

Abanazir, Cem. 2018. Institutionalisation in E-Sports. *Sport, Ethics and Philosophy* 1–15. Accessed 2 November 2018. https://doi.org/10.1080/1751 1321.2018.1453538.

Adamus, Tanja. 2012. Playing Computer Games as Electronic Sport: In Search of a Theoretical Framework for a New Research Field. In *Computer Games and New Media Cultures: A Handbook of Digital Game Studies*, ed. Johannes Fromme and Alexander Unger, 477–490. Dordrecht: Springer.

Adler, Nancy, and Allison Gundersen. 2007. *International Dimensions of Organizational Behavior*. 8th ed. Mason, OH: Thompson Higher Education.

Adomnica, Marius 2017. Is Blizzard Killing Overwatch as an E-Sport? Accessed 2 November 2018. https://thepatchnotes.com/2017/06/22/is-blizzard-killing-overwatch.

———. 2018. Blizzard Starting to Shut Down Hearthstone Fan Leagues—How Will Community React? Accessed 2 November 2018. https://thepatchnotes. com/2018/10/17/blizzard-starting-to-shut-down-hearthstone-fan-leagues-do-your-worst-community.

Alvarez, Edgar. 2018. Even the World Cup Couldn't Escape the 'Fortnite' Fever. Accessed 2 November 2018. https://www.engadget.com/2018/07/14/world-cup-goals-fortnite-dance-celebrations.

Apesteguia, Jose, Ghazala Azmat, and Nagore Iriberri. 2012. The Impact of Gender Composition on Team Performance and Decision Making: Evidence from the Field. *Management Science* 58 (1): 78–93.

Asarch, Steven. 2018. How Blizzard Helped Pioneer Esports Without Realizing It. Accessed 2 November 2018. https://www.newsweek.com/2018/08/24/blizzard-overwatch-ceo-StarCraft-mike-morhaime-esports-1075317.html.

Ashton, Graham. 2018a. Does Counter-Strike Need Its Own Version of the International? Accessed 2 November 2018. https://esportsobserver.com/does-csgo-need-international.

———. 2018b. McDonald's Parts Ways with German Soccer, Doubles Down on Esports. Accessed 2 November 2018. https://esportsobserver.com/mcdonalds-esl-deal-renewal.

———. 2018c. Stefan Zant, ProSiebenSat.1 Sports—'There is a Huge Audience Out There Which Doesn't Have Seven Hours to Watch a Live Even'. Accessed 2 November 2018. https://esportsobserver.com/stefan-zant-interview-prosieben.

Azevedo, Mary Ann. 2018. Esports Continues To Go Mainstream as Funding Surges In 2018. Accessed 2 November 2018. https://news.crunchbase.com/news/esports-continues-to-go-mainstream-as-funding-surges-in-2018.

Baccellieri, Emma. 2018. Report: Twitch Signs Two-Year Deal With Overwatch League Worth at Least $90 Million. Accessed 2 November 2018. https://compete.kotaku.com/report-twitch-signs-two-year-deal-with-overwatch-leagu-1821932438.

Ballantyne, Erica E.F., Maria Lindholm, and Anthony Whiteing. 2013. A Comparative Study of Urban Freight Transport Planning: Addressing Stakeholder Needs. *Journal of Transport Geography* 32: 93–101.

Berc, Lucas. 2018. Ninjas in Pyjamas and Betway Extend the Partnership. Accessed 2 November 2018. https://nip.gl/article/ninjas-in-pyjamas-and-betway-extend-the-partnership.

Besombes, Nicolas. 2018. Tweet. Accessed 2 November 2018. https://twitter.com/NicoBesombes/status/1009123040955850752.

Bevir, Mark. 2012. *Governance: A Very Short Introduction.* Oxford: Oxford University Press.

Booker, Logan. 2018. Top 10 Twitch Streamer Reveals How Much They Make From Donations, Ads, Subs And Sponsorships. Accessed 2 November 2018. https://www.kotaku.com.au/2018/10/top-10-twitch-streamer-reveals-how-much-they-make-from-donations-ads-subs-and-sponsorships.

Brock, Tom, and Emma Fraser. 2018. Is Computer Gaming a Craft? Prehension, Practice, and Puzzle-Solving in Gaming Labour. *Information, Communication & Society* 21 (9): 1219–1233.

Brugha, Ruairi, and Zuszsa Varvasovszky. 2000. Stakeholder Analysis: A Review. *Health Policy and Planning* 15 (3): 239–246.

Bryson, John M. 2004. What to Do When Stakeholders Matter: Stakeholder Identification and Analysis Techniques. *Public Management Review* 6 (1): 21–53.

Byers, Preston. 2018. Activision Blizzard has Reportedly Offered Call of Duty Franchise Slots to Overwatch League Teams. Accessed 2 November 2018. https://dotesports.com/call-of-duty/news/activision-blizzard-has-reportedly-offered-call-of-duty-franchise-slots-to-overwatch-league-teams.

Campbell, Colin. 2016. Life is Though on the Counter-Strike Pro Circuit. Accessed 2 November 2018. https://www.polygon.com/2016/4/12/11388750/cs-gold-rush.

Cardador, M. Teresa, Gregory B. Northcraft, and Jordan Whicker. 2017. A Theory of Work Gamification: Something Old, Something New, Something Borrowed, Something Cool? *Human Resource Management Review* 27 (2): 353–365.

Carp, Sam. 2018. Nike Names Jian Zihao as First Esports Ambassador. Accessed 2 November 2018. http://www.sportspromedia.com/news/nike-jian-zihao-esports-endorsement-lebron-james.

Carpenter, Nicole. 2018a. LFT OWL: Inside Overwatch League's Off-Season. Accessed 2 November 2018. https://dotesports.com/overwatch/news/lft-owl-inside-overwatch-leagues-off-season.

———. 2018b. Houston Outlaws Coach Let Go Amid Ongoing Infinite Esports Layoffs. Accessed 2 November 2018. https://dotesports.com/overwatch/news/houston-outlaws-coach-let-go-amid-ongoing-infinite-esports-layoffs.

———. 2018c. A Blurred Line Between Work and Play Could Cause Trouble for the Overwatch League. Accessed 2 November 2018. https://dotesports.com/overwatch/news/player-health-burnout-ow-league-23993.

Castronova, Edward. 2005. *Synthetic Worlds: The Business and Culture of Online Games*. Chicago: University of Chicago Press.

Chalk, Andy. 2015. Valve Bans Seven CS:GO Pro Players from Tournament Play for Match Fixing. Accessed 2 November 2018. https://www.pcgamer.com/valve-suspends-seven-csgo-pro-players-for-match-fixing.

Chao, Laura L. 2017. 'You Must Construct Additional Pylons': Building a Better Framework for Esports Governance. *Fordham Law Review* 86 (2): 737–765.

Christou, Luke. 2018. Faker Salary: How Much Does SKT's Faker Make? Accessed 2 November 2018. https://finalkill.com/league-of-legends/faker-salary.

Cocke, Taylor. 2018a. How Do You Best Monetize an Audience? Esports Team Execs Weigh In. Accessed 2 November 2018. https://esportsobserver.com/hive-recap-esports-organization-recap.

———. 2018b. Cuts at Infinite Esports and Echo Fox Signal an Esports Correction, Not Trouble. Accessed 2 November 2018. https://esportsobserver.com/infinite-esports-echo-fox-cuts.

Cooke, Sam. 2017. Olympique Lyonnais Launch FIFA Esports Team in Beijing. Accessed 2 November 2018. http://www.esportsinsider.com/2017/03/olympique-lyonnais-launch-fifa-esports-team-beijing.

Cunningham, George B., Sheranne Fairley, Lesley Ferkins, Shannon Kerwin, Daniel Lock, Sally Shaw, and Pamela Wicker. 2018. eSport: Construct Specifications and Implications for Sport Management. *Sport Management Review* 21 (1): 1–6.

D'Orazio, Nick. 2018a. Seagull Retires from the Overwatch League to Stream Full Time. Accessed 2 November 2018. https://www.invenglobal.com/articles/5878/seagull-retires-from-the-overwatch-league-to-stream-full-time.

———. 2018b. Overwatch League Players are Tired. Accessed 2 November 2018. https://www.invenglobal.com/articles/5957/overwatch-league-players-are-tired.

Darnall, Nicole, Irene Henriques, and Perry Sadorsky. 2010. Adopting Proactive Environmental Strategy: The Influence of Stakeholders and Firm Size. *Journal of Management Studies* 47 (6): 1072–1094.

Deloitte. 2018. Deloitte nieuwe partner ESL Dutch Championship. Accessed 2 November 2018. https://www2.deloitte.com/nl/nl/pages/over-deloitte/articles/deloitte-nieuwe-partner-esl-dutch-championship.html.

Eesley, Charles, and Michael J. Lenox. 2006. Firm Responses to Secondary Stakeholder Action. *Strategic Management Journal* 27 (8): 765–781.

Ejiochi, Ike. 2014. How the NFL Makes the Most Money of Any Pro Sport. Accessed 2 November 2018. https://www.cnbc.com/2014/09/04/how-the-nfl-makes-the-most-money-of-any-pro-sport.html.

Elsam, Sara. 2018. Tim Reichert, FC Schalke 04 Esports—Traditional Teams Need to Approach Esports in a 'Bigger Way'. Accessed 2 November 2018. https://esportsobserver.com/tim-reichert-schalke-04-interview.

ESC.watch. 2018a. Overwatch Contenders 2018 Season 1: China. Accessed 2 November 2018. https://esc.watch/tournaments/ow/owc-2018-china.

————. 2018b. Tom Clancy's Rainbow Six Siege. Accessed 2 November 2018. https://esc.watch/tournaments/rainbow-6.

ESIC. 2016. *Threats to the Integrity of Esports. A Risk Analysis.* Cologne: ESIC.

ESPN. 2017. Confidential: Life as a League of Legends Pro. Accessed 2 November 2018. http://www.espn.com/esports/story/_/id/18461870/life-league-legends-pro.

Eventbrite. 2015. *The eSports Effect: Gamers and the Influence of Live Events.* London: Eventbrite.

Fischer, Ben. 2018. Overwatch League to Cut Season Length, Hoping to Give Teams More Marketing Time. Accessed 2 November 2018. https://esportsobserver.com/owl-cuts-season-length.

Fitch, Adam. 2018. Seoul Dynasty Allegedly Block London Spitfire from Visiting Fans. Accessed 2 November 2018. https://cybersport.com/post/london-spitfire-cant-visit-seoul.

Fletcher, Anne, James Guthrie, Peter Steane, Göran Roos, and Stephen Pike. 2003. Mapping Stakeholder Perceptions for a Third Sector Organization. *Journal of Intellectual Capital* 4 (4): 505–527.

Forbes. 2018. Forbes Releases 20th Annual NBA Team Valuations. Accessed 2 November 2018. https://www.forbes.com/sites/forbespr/2018/02/07/forbes-releases-20th-annual-nba-team-valuations/#1c6b8fd434e6.

Franke, Tilo. 2015. The Perception of eSports—Mainstream Culture, Real Sport and Marketisation. In *eSports Yearbook 2013/14*, ed. Julia Hiltscher and Tobias M. Scholz, 111–144. Norderstedt, Germany: Books on Demand.

Freeman, R. Edward, and David L. Reed. 1983. Stockholders and Stakeholders: A New Perspective on Corporate Governance. *California Management Review* 25 (3): 88–106.

Freeman, R. Edward. 1984. *Strategic Management: A Stakeholder Approach.* Boston: Pitman.

————. 1994. The Politics of Stakeholder Theory: Some Future Directions. *Business Ethics Quarterly* 4 (4): 409–421.

GAISF. n.d. Mission and Vision. Accessed 2 November 2018. https://gaisf.sport/mission-and-vision.

Giannacco, Carlo. 2015. Farewell Message Cloud. In *eSports Yearbook 2013/14*, ed. Julia Hiltscher and Tobias M. Scholz, 89–92. Norderstedt, Germany: Books on Demand.

Goldhaber, Ben. 2018. Tweet. Accessed 2 November 2018. https://twitter.com/FishStix/status/1049777937820528641.

Gray, H.L. 1978. The Entrepreneurial Innovator. *Management Learning* 9 (2): 85–92.

Gurdus, Elizabeth. 2018. It's 'Inevitable' that Esports Will Be Part of the Olympics, Logitech CEO Say. Accessed 2 November 2018. https://www.cnbc.com/2018/08/07/logitech-ceo-its-inevitable-that-esports-will-be-part-of-olympics.html.

Hallmann, Kirstin, and Thomas Giel. 2018. eSports—Competitive Sports or Recreational Activity? *Sport Management Review* 21 (1): 14–20.

Hebbel-Seeger, Andreas. 2012. The Relationship Between Real Sports and Digital Adaptation in E-Sport Gaming. *International Journal of Sports Marketing & Sponsorship* 13 (2): 132–143.

Hippeau, Lerer. 2018. What Investors Should Know About the Rise of eSports Betting. Accessed 2 November 2018. https://medium.com/@LererHippeau/what-investors-should-know-about-the-rise-of-esports-betting-34e1685f49ae.

Holden, John T., Anastasios Kaburakis, and Ryan Rodenberg. 2017a. The Future is Now: eSports Policy Considerations and Potential Litigation. *Journal of Legal Aspects of Sport* 27 (1): 46–78.

Holden, John T., Ryan M. Rodenberg, and Anastasios Kaburakis. 2017b. Esports Corruption: Gambling, Doping, and Global Governance. *Maryland Journal of International Law* 32 (1): 236–273.

Hollist, Katherine E. 2016. Time to Be Grown-Ups About Video Gaming: The Rising eSports Industry and the Need for Regulation. *Arizona Law Review* 57: 823–847.

Hutchins, Brett. 2008. Signs of Meta-Change in Second Modernity: The Growth of E-Sport and the World Cyber Games. *New Media & Society* 10 (6): 851–869.

Jenny, Seth E., Margaret C. Keiper, Blake J. Taylor, Dylan P. Williams, Garysiak Joey, R. Douglas Manning, and Patrick M. Tutka. 2018. eSports Venues. A New Sport Business Opportunity. *Journal of Applied Sport Management* 10 (1): 34–49.

Jenny, Seth E., R. Douglas Manning, Margaret C. Keiper, and Tracy W. Olrich. 2017. Virtual(ly) Athletes: Where eSports Fit Within the Definition of 'Sport'. *Quest* 69 (1): 1–18.

JKCP. 2018. How Much Do Pro Gamers & Esports Players Make? Accessed 2 November 2018. https://info.jkcp.com/blog/professional-gamer-salary-esports.

Jonasson, Kalle, and Jesper Thiborg. 2010. Electronic Sport and Its Impact on Future Sport. *Sport in Society* 13 (2): 287–299.

Jordan, Markus. 2018. Mercedes-Benz erweitert Partnerschaft mit ESL. Accessed 2 November 2018. https://blog.mercedes-benz-passion.com/2018/10/mercedes-benz-erweitert-partnerschaft-mit-esl.

Kain, Erik. 2018. Amazon's Terrible Twitch Prime Changes Should Make You Consider Unsubscribing. Accessed 2 November 2018. https://www.forbes.com/sites/erikkain/2018/08/21/amazons-terrible-twitch-prime-changes-should-make-you-angry.

Keiper, Margaret C., R. Douglas Manning, Seth Jenny, Tracy Olrich, and Chris Croft. 2017. No Reason to LoL at LoL: The Addition of Esports to Intercollegiate Athletic Departments. *Journal for the Study of Sports and Athletes in Education* 11 (2): 143–160.

Komplett. 2017. Accessed 2 November 2018. https://www.komplett.no/kampanje/32959/gaming/esport-i-rask-vekst.

Koueider, Adam. 2018. Interview with OpTic's LoL General Manager Romain. Accessed 2 November 2018. https://www.liquidlegends.net/forum/lol-general/531576-interview-with-optics-lol-general-manager-romain.

Kücklich, Julian. 2005. Precarious Playbour: Modders and the Digital Games Industry. *Fibreculture* 3. Accessed 2 November 2018. http://five.fibreculture-journal.org/fcj-025-precarious-playbour-modders-and-the-digital-games-industry.

Kutateladze, Artyom. 2018. StarLadder to Launch the First €1,000,000 European PUBG Pro League. Accessed 2 November 2018. https://cybersport.com/post/starladder-first-european-pubg-pro-league.

Lewis, Leo, and Tim Bradshaw 2017. Esports: Is the Gaming Business Ready to Come of Age? Accessed 2 November 2018. https://www.ft.com/content/ef8539b6-be2a-11e7-9836-b25f8adaa111.

Lewis, Richard. 2018a. Exclusive: Recording of Meeting Regarding Contenders Surfaces, Confirms Downsizing. Accessed 2 November 2018. https://www.vpesports.com/overwatch/exclusive-recording-of-meeting-regarding-contenders-surfaces-confirms-downsizing.

———. 2018b. Richard Lewis at the ESIC, 'Money Flooding into Sports Has, Naturally, Brought with It Corruption at All Levels'. Accessed 2 November 2018. https://www.vpesports.com/more-esports/richard-lewis-at-the-esic-money-flooding-into-sports-has-naturally-brought-with-it-corruption-at-all-levels.

Li, Xing. 2018. What Role Should Outside Capital Play in Esports. Accessed 2 November 2018. https://dotesports.com/business/news/role-venture-capital-esports-29540.

Lin, Tom C.W. 2011. The Corporate Governance of Iconic Executives. *Notre Dame Law Review* 87 (1): 351–382.

Lippe, Richard, and Susan Tully. 2017. H2k's Letter to the EU LCS Community. Accessed 2 November 2018. http://h2k.gg/story/h2ks-letter-to-the-eu-lcs-community.

Lombardo, John and David Broughton. 2017. Going Gray. Sports TV Viewers Skew Older. Accessed 2 November 2018. http://www.sportsbusinessdaily.com/Journal/Issues/2017/06/05/Research-and-Ratings/Viewership-trends.aspx.

Macey, Joseph, and Juho Hamari. 2018. Investigating Relationships Between Video Gaming, Spectating Esports, and Gambling. *Computers in Human Behavior* 80: 344–353.

Mallant, Jos. 2017. About EU—Problems and Future. Accessed 2 November 2018. https://www.unicornsofloveapp.com/news/c/0/i/17477178/about-eu-problems-and-future.

Massaad, Jay. 2017. The 2018 OWL and NA LCS Ownership Guide. Accessed 2 November 2018. https://esportsinsider.com/2017/12/2018-owl-na-lcs-ownership-guide.

Mastercard. 2018. Mastercard Signs with League of Legends as First Global Partner of the World's Largest Esport. Accessed 2 November 2018. https://newsroom.mastercard.com/press-releases/mastercard-signs-with-league-of-legends-as-first-global-partner-of-the-worlds-largest-esport.

McMillan, Scott. 2018. Tweet. Accessed 2 November 2018. https://www.twitter.com/Methodsco/status/1042534267593601024.

Miceli, Max. 2018a. Why Esports Organizations are Recruiting Large Fortnite Teams. Accessed 2 November 2018. https://esportsobserver.com/why-esports-organizations-are-recruiting-large-fortnite-teams.

———. 2018b. ESL's Michal Blicharz Discusses Esports' Olympic Hopes Following IOC Forum. Accessed 2 November 2018. https://esportsobserver.com/michal-carmac-blicharz-esl-olympics.

Mickunas, Aaron. 2018. Riot's Relationship with Tencent Has Reportedly Been Strained Over Declining Profits and Mobile Games. Accessed 2 November 2018. https://dotesports.com/league-of-legends/news/riot-strained-relationship-tencent-declining-players-mobile-games-information-32079.

Mitchell, Ferguson. 2018. Why Brands & Influencers are Taking Center Stage in Esports. Accessed 2 November 2018. https://esportsobserver.com/brands-esports-sponsorship-growth.

MTG. 2018. MTG Increases Ownership in ESL & Writes Down Zoomin.TV Assets. Accessed 2 November 2018. https://www.mtg.com/press-releases/mtg-increases-ownership-in-esl-writes-down-zoomin-tv-assets.

Murray, Trent. 2018a. Rainbow Six Moves to League Format, But Stays True to Its Methodical Growth Strategy. Accessed 2 November 2018. https://esportsobserver.com/rainbow-six-esports-potential.

———. 2018b. James Lampkin, ESL VP of Product on Surviving as a Third Party Organizer in a World of First Party Leagues. Accessed 2 November 2018. https://esportsobserver.com/interview-james-lampkin-esl.

———. 2018c. Vancouver Overwatch League Team Names Luminosity as Operations Partner. Accessed 2 November 2018. https://esportsobserver.com/vancouver-overwatch-luminosity-partner.

Nanzer, Nate. 2018. Overwatch League: E-Sports Done Differently. Accessed 2 November 2018. https://youtu.be/Ep1YWc-4eA0.

Newell, Adam. 2018. How Much Does Faker Make? Accessed 2 November 2018. https://dotsports.com/league-of-legends/news/faker-earnings-league-of-legends-14357.

Nordmark, Sam. 2018. How Advertising in Esports is Changing. Accessed 2 November 2018. https://dotsports.com/general/news/how-advertising-in-esports-is-changing.

OECD. 2004. OECD Principles of Corporate Governance. Accessed 2 November 2018. http://www.oecd.org/corporate/ca/corporategovernance-principles/31557724.pdf.

Oprescu, Florin, Christian Jones, and Mary Katsikitis. 2014. I Play at Work— Ten Principles for Transforming Work Processes Trough Gamification. *Frontiers in Psychology* 5: 1–5.

Parry, Jim. 2018. E-Sports are Not Sports. *Sport, Ethics and Philosophy*. Accessed 2 November 2018. https://doi.org/10.1080/17511321.2018.1489419.

Partin, Will. 2018a. Blizzard's Ban on Third-Party Overwatch Apps Was Never About Competitive Integrity. Accessed 2 November 2018. https://variety.com/2018/gaming/columns/blizzards-ban-on-third-party-overwatch-apps-was-never-about-competitive-integrity-1202961745.

———. 2018b. 'StarCraft II': How Blizzard Brought the King of Esports Back From the Dead. Accessed 2 November 2018. https://variety.com/2018/gaming/features/StarCraft-ii-esports-history-1202873246.

Pei, Annie. 2018. South Korea Esports Network OGN to Invest at Least $100 Million in North America, Plans Big Partnership with Battle Royale Giant

PUBG. Accessed 2 November 2018. https://www.cnbc.com/2018/10/10/esports-network-ogn-to-invest-at-least-100-million-in-north-america.html.

Porter, Michael E. 1985. *Competitive Advantage: Creating and Sustaining Superior Performance*. New York: Simon and Schuster.

PSG. 2017. We are Withdrawing from League of Legends for Now. Accessed 2 November 2018. https://psg-esports.com/we-are-withdrawing-from-league-of-legends-for-now.

PwC. 2018. *Sports Industry: Lost in Transition. PwC's Sport Survey 2018*. Zurich: PwC.

Randhawa, Navneet. 2015. The Games, the Audience, and the Performance. In *eSports Yearbook 2013/14*, ed. Julia Hiltscher and Tobias M. Scholz, 15–22. Norderstedt, Germany: Books on Demand.

Reimer, Jeremy. 2011. The Dawn of Starcraft: e-Sports Come to the World Stage. Accessed 2 November 2018. https://arstechnica.com/gaming/2011/03/the-dawn-of-StarCraft-e-sports-come-to-the-world-stage.

Reuters. 2018. Olympics. E-Sports Could Be Sports Activity. Accessed 2 November 2018. https://www.reuters.com/article/us-olympics-summit/olympics-e-sports-could-be-sports-activity-says-ioc-idUSKBN1CX0IR.

Reynolds, Scott J., Frank C. Schultz, and David R. Hekman. 2006. Stakeholder Theory and Managerial Decision-Making: Constraints and Implications of Balancing Stakeholder Interests. *Journal of Business Ethics* 64 (3): 285–301.

Riot. n.d. Accessed 2 November 2018. https://na.leagueoflegends.com/en/news/game-updates.

Rizzo, Tim. 2018. Blizzard's Investment in Heroes Esports is an Investment in the Games Future. Accessed 2 November 2018. https://www.invenglobal.com/articles/5132/blizzards-investment-in-heroes-esports-is-an-investment-in-the-games-future.

Roberts, Craig. 2018. 'Going Long': Which Sports Would You Buy on a Global Exchange. Accessed 2 November 2018. http://thegembagroup.com/news/going-long-sports-buy-global-exchange.

Rogers, Jacob. 2012. Crafting an Industry: An Analysis of Korean StarCraft and Intellectual Properties Law. Accessed 2 November 2018. https://jolt.law.harvard.edu/digest/crafting-an-industry-an-analysis-of-korean-starcraft-and-intellectual-properties-law.

Rohan. 2018. The CSPPA is a Necessity as Esports Grows, Better Late than Never. Accessed 2 November 2018. https://esports-betting-tips.com/the-csppa-is-a-necessity-as-esports-grows-better-late-than-never.

Rosa, Jeremy. 2018. Esports: What is It and is It Real. Accessed 2 November 2018. http://blogs.ci.com/harbour/jeremy-rosa/esports-what-it-and-it-real.

Rosell Llorens, Mariona. 2017. eSport Gaming: The Rise of a New Sports Practice. *Sport, Ethics and Philosophy* 11 (4): 464–476.

Savage, Grant T., Timothy W. Nix, Carlton J. Whitehead, and John D. Blair. 1991. Strategies for Assessing and Managing Organizational Stakeholders. *Academy of Management Perspectives* 5 (2): 61–75.

Schenkhuizen, Manuel. 2013. Manifesto on SC2 eSports. In *eSports Yearbook 2011/12*, ed. Julia Christophers and Tobias M. Scholz, 26–32. Norderstedt, Germany: Books on Demand.

Schilling, Frieder. 2016. Warum Schalke ein eSport-Team für 'League of Legends' kauft. Accessed 2 November 2018. http://www.manager-magazin. de/unternehmen/artikel/esport-fc-schalke-04-kauft-profis-fuer-league-of-legends-in-der-lcs-a-1112424.html.

Schmidt, Sascha L., and Florian Holzmayer. 2018a. A Framework for Diversification Decisions in Professional Football. In *Routledge Handbook of Football Business and Management*, ed. Simon Chadwick, Daniel Parnell, Paul Widdop, and Christos Anagnostopoulos, 3–19. London: Routledge.

———. 2018b. FC Schalke 04 Esports. Decision Making in a Changing Ecosystem. *WHU Publishing Case Number CSM-0001*: 1–21.

Scholz, Tobias M. 2012. Talent Management in the Video Game Industry: The Role of Cultural Diversity and Cultural Intelligence. *Thunderbird International Business Review* 54 (6): 845–858.

———. 2015. Game Leadership—What Can We Learn from Competitive Games? In *eSports Yearbook 2013/14*, ed. Julia Hiltscher and Tobias M. Scholz, 93–106. Norderstedt, Germany: Books on Demand.

Scholz, Tobias M., and Volker Stein. 2017. Going Beyond Ambidexterity in the Media Industry: eSports as Pioneer of Ultradexterity. *International Journal of Gaming and Computer-Mediated Simulations* 9 (2): 47–62.

Schultz, E.J. 2017. A How-To-Guide for Esports Branding. Accessed 2 November 2018. https://adage.com/article/news/guide-esports-branding/308502.

Seeger, Britta. 2018. Sponsoring in Esports: Mercedes-Benz Expands Partnership with ESL. Accessed 2 November 2018. https://media.daimler.com/marsMediaSite/en/instance/ko/Sponsoring-in-esports-Mercedes-Benz-expands-partnership-with-ESL.xhtml?oid=41570448.

Shaw, Adrienne. 2010. What is Video Game Culture? Cultural Studies and Game Studies. *Games and Culture* 5 (4): 403–424.

Sinclair. 2015. 12 Arrested in eSports Match Fixing Scandal. Accessed 2 November 2018. https://www.gamesindustry.biz/articles/2015-10-19-12-arrested-in-esports-match-fixing-scandal-report.

Sjöblom, Max, and Juho Hamari. 2017. Why Do People Watch Others Play Video Games? An Empirical Study on the Motivations of Twitch Users. *Computers in Human Behavior* 75: 985–996.

Smith, Scott. 2018. Tweet. Accessed 2 November 2018. https://twitter.com/SirScoots/status/1053323392521302016?s=20.

Spiegel. 2018. Die Favoriten auf den League-of-Legends-Titel. Accessed 2 November 2018. http://www.spiegel.de/sport/sonst/league-of-legends-die-favoriten-bei-den-worlds-2018-a-1234088.html.

Sponsors. 2018. Studie: Das sind die bekanntesten eSport-Sponsoren. Accessed 2 November 2018. https://www.sponsors.de/news/sponsoring/studie-das-sind-die-bekanntesten-esport-sponsoren.

Stein, Volker, and Tobias M. Scholz. 2016. The Intercultural Challenge of Building the European eSports League for Video Gaming. In *Intercultural Management: A Case-Based Approach to Achieving Complementarity and Synergy*, ed. Christoph Barmeyer and Peter Franklin, 80–94. London: Palgrave.

Superdata. 2015. *eSports—The Market Brief 2015*. New York: Superdata.

———. 2018. *Esports Courtside: Playmakers of 2017*. New York: Superdata.

Svensson, Göran. 2001. 'Glocalization' of Business Activities: A 'Glocal Strategy' Approach. *Management Decision* 39 (1): 6–18.

Taylor, T.L. 2012. *Raising the Stakes: E-sports and the Professionalization of Computer Gaming*. Cambridge, MA: MIT Press.

———. 2018. *Watch Me Play. Twitch and the Rise of Game Live Streaming*. Princeton, NJ and Oxford: Princeton University Press.

Thompson, Barney. 2015. Let the Egames Begin. Accessed 2 November 2018. http://www.ft.com/cms/s/2/64bfe382-412f-11e5-9abe-5b335da3a90e.html#axzz3qW0SLgLi.

Tielbeke, Alex. 2017. Eredivisie Launches Official Esports Competition for Fifa Gamers: The E-Divisie. Accessed 2 November 2018. https://eredivisie.nl/nl-nl/nieuwsbericht/eredivisie-launches-official-esports-competition-for-fifa-gamers-the-edivisie.

Tushman, Michael L., and Ralph Katz. 1980. External Communication and Project Performance: An Investigation into the Role of Gatekeepers. *Management Science* 26 (11): 1071–1085.

UNESCO. n.d. Concept of Governance. Accessed 2 November 2018. http://www.ibe.unesco.org/en/geqaf/technical-notes/concept-governance.

Valentine, Rebekah. 2018. Nate Nanzer: 'The Train Has Left the Station' on Esports Opportunities. Accessed 2 November 2018. https://www.gamesindustry.biz/articles/2018-09-27-nate-nanzer-the-train-has-left-the-station-on-esports-opportunities.

van der Sar, Edwin. (2016). Nederlands beste FIFA E-Sporter Koen Weijland tekent bij Ajax. Accessed 2 November 2018. https://www.ajax.nl/streams/actueel/nederlands-beste-fifa-esporter-koen-weijland-tekent-bij-ajax.htm.

Volk, Pete. 2016. Rick Fox on Echo Fox, the Growth of Esports and His Budding Rivalry with Shaq. Accessed 2 November 2018. http://www.riftherald.com/interviews/2016/6/2/11829364/rick-fox-echo-fox-esports-interview.

Volkov, Daniil. 2018. EU LCS Franchising: A Fading Spark. Accessed 2 November 2018. https://realsport101.com/news/sports/esports/league-of-legends/eu-lcs-franchising-a-fading-spark.

Webster, Andrew. 2018. Why Competitive Gaming is Starting to Look a Lot like Professional Sports. Accessed 2 November 2018. https://www.theverge.com/2018/7/27/17616532/overwatch-league-of-legends-nba-nfl-esports.

Weiss, Thomas, and Sabrina Schiele. 2013. Virtual Worlds in Competitive Contexts: Analyzing eSports Consumer Needs. *Electronic Markets* 23 (4): 307–316.

Weststar, Johanna. 2015. Understanding Video Game Developers as an Occupational Community. *Information, Communication & Society* 18 (10): 1238–1252.

Williams, Rob. 2018. The IOC is Considering Including eSports in the Olympic Games. Accessed 2 November 2018. http://dailyhive.com/toronto/video-games-esports-olympics.

Witkowski, Emma. 2010. Probing the Sportiness of eSports. In *eSports Yearbook 2009*, ed. Julia Christophers and Tobias M. Scholz, 53–56. Norderstedt, Germany: Books on Demand.

Wolf, Jacob. 2017. Blizzard Entertainment Locks in Two More $20 Million Overwatch League Spots. Accessed 2 November 2018. http://www.espn.com/esports/story/_/id/20673359/blizzard-entertainment-locks-two-more-20-million-overwatch-league-spots.

Woodcock, Jamie, and Mark R. Johnson. 2018. Work, Play, and Precariousness: An Overview of the Labour Ecosystem of Esports. Working Paper.

WSF. n.d. About. Accessed 2 November 2018. http://worldskateboardingfederation.org/about.

Youngmisuk, Ohm, and Jacob Wolf. 2018. How Adam Silver Made His Mark on Esports in North America. Accessed 2 November 2018. http://www.espn.com/esports/story/_/id/23006808/how-adam-silver-made-mark-esports-north-america.

Zacny, Rob. 2017. 'Dota 2' Owes Its Success to Fans, Not Investors and Owners, and That's Okay. Accessed 2 November 2018. https://waypoint.vice.com/en_us/article/ae5w88/dota-2-owes-its-success-to-fans-not-investors-and-owners-and-thats-okay.

4

Unwritten Governing Principles

Abstract Based on the long eSports history and the interaction of the stakeholders, it becomes evident that eSports follows certain principles, although they are unwritten, and reviewing the management decisions in the past reveals these principles. These principles are derived and institutionalized over time and show self-governance within eSports. The roots of eSports are influenced by concepts like 'easy to learn, hard to master', the shifting metagame, and the game design. The Wild West metaphor is an ongoing motif, but a more in-depth observation highlights its potential influence. The principle of born digital, born global, and born agile explains the uniqueness of eSports, being an industry that is by its nature part of a digitized, global, and agile world.

Keywords eSports • eSports industry • Governing principles • Social constructivism • eSports culture • Strategic management

The Creation and Solidification of Governing Principles

The eSports environment is highly complex and highly diverse. Many stakeholders are involved and are trying to foster growth for themselves, as well as for the eSports industry in its entirety. However, with the absence of one unified governing body and a decentralization of power, no unified consensus can describe the eSports industry. More importantly, without one governing body, there is an ongoing debate about what eSports is. However, these discussions are often carried out on a visible level and mostly focus on surface features that everybody can observe. The eSports industry is, however, unique in its composition and how the stakeholders act with each other, primarily as they are highly interwoven. Even though the surface may seem quite diverse, the invisible level shines through, and certain governing principles can be discovered.

The assumption that there is a visible level consisting of symbols, rituals, and people, as well as the assumption that there is an invisible level consisting of values, beliefs, and basic presumptions, is a prevailing theory concerning organizational culture. Schein's (1985) iceberg model highlights the importance of digging deeper into the culture of an organization. The basic underlying assumptions are difficult to decipher; however, they will influence the observable behavior and, even though they are unconscious, they are often taken for granted by the people involved in this organization. This understanding of culture can be translated to the eSports industry, which has a distinct organizational culture.

In contrast to a finite corporation, the eSports industry as an organization is influenced by the variety of its stakeholders, and there is a lack of unified symbols—or, as Schein defined them artifacts—but there is no lack of values and underlying assumptions. However, without a governing body having the power to influence this development, the emergence of values and underlying assumptions is a social phenomenon and evolution. In the social sciences, the concept of social constructivism is an explanation for the process of creating such shared values in a group of people. The most defining work on social constructivism was written by Berger and Luckmann in 1966. They categorize reality into a subjective reality and an objective reality. However, for them, 'objective' does not have the same meaning as 'objectivity': "It is important to keep in mind that the objectivity of the institutional world, however massive it may appear to the individual, is a humanly produced, constructed objectivity" (Berger and Luckmann 1966, p. 60) and, more concisely, "society is a human product" (Berger and Luckmann 1966, p. 61). Reality is, therefore, a construction of the individual; consequently, social interaction will lead to a mutually shaped social reality.

Berger and Luckmann (1966) categorize this process in three phases: the habitualization, the institutionalization, and the legitimation. The habitualization is based on social interaction: a group of people create a preliminary consensus and establish a particular set of norms, and through ongoing repetition this is shared with other social groups. If this set of social norms is continually shared with and by others, it becomes institutionalized. It is important to highlight that institutionalization does not mean the emergence of institutions, but rather the alignment into a shared set of norms, rules, symbols, or even language. The case of language can be observed in eSports with a distinct set of words that are unilaterally shared with everybody (e.g., the term 'noob'). This institutionalization is further fortified through the process of legitimation, in which these shared beliefs and values become an essential part of the unified assumptions, mainly due to their utilization by dominant social groups. Again, the wording of eSports is a perfect example of ongoing social constructivism and, maybe in the future, a reality will be created in which the discussion is finished and a unified style adapted.

Although eSports is often seen as a young and emerging industry, there is a large corpus of history concerning eSports. In its modern form, driven by technological progress and innovations, it is possible to identify specific patterns that have been repeated. Based on that knowledge, and the analysis of the history of eSports, the following governing principles are proposed: (1) easy to learn, hard to master; (2) shifting metagame; (3) welcome to the Wild West; and (4) born digital, born global, born agile. These governing principles allow a better understanding of the eSports industry and can act as basic assumptions that are shared by the eSports industry. However, as it is a volatile industry, there are also shifts in these governing principles, as well as stakeholders revolting against these principles. Still, many behaviors of many stakeholders can be described by these principles.

Easy to Learn, Hard to Master

The first governing principle is derived from video game design and can also be described as one of the cornerstones of video game design. The so-called Bushnell's law or Nolan's law contends that "All the best games are easy to learn and difficult to master. They should reward the first quarter and the hundredth" (Bogost 2009). Companies like Activision Blizzard see this law as a driving force for their game design, and in video games like *World of Warcraft*, this design principle becomes especially apparent. Starting the game is relatively easy, and the player will experience a steady learning curve, but the top level is challenging for the players to reach (Cifaldi 2010). In November 2018, fewer than 200 guilds—which is only a small fraction—have beaten the hardest content in the game, the Uldir raid (WoWProgress 2018). This game design concept can be observed in any successful eSports title. It is simple to learn the game, to understand the game, and to have some fun, but becoming the very best is extremely difficult and requires talent and passion. Games like *League of Legends*, *Counter-Strike*, *Overwatch*, and many other titles work on the easy to learn part as well as the hard to master, making it a governing principle for any video game developer.

But this principle is also important for the various stakeholders in the eSports industry. First of all, easy to learn also means that the game may be easy to watch and easy to understand. The significant advantage of MOBA titles like *League of Legends* or *Dota 2* is that the audience can follow the game, even though they may have never played the game. Other games like *Overwatch* or, more obviously, *World of Warcraft* may be easy for the player to learn, but watching these games is difficult. *World of Warcraft* faced the challenge of making a game watchable for a broad audience; although millions play the game, watching PvP tournaments is difficult, even for the experts in the game. The principle easy to learn to observe is also increasingly important, as many people watch various eSports titles and try to follow all of those leagues and tournaments. For tournament operators, this may even be a way to keep the offline audience interested by switching between various games. The reason that *StarCraft II* has become popular again in recent years is that it is a game that can co-exist with other games (Blicharz, cited in Partin 2018a). Cross-border viewing is a necessary part of content creation and allows players, teams, and tournament operators to utilize potential synergetic effects.

Additionally, easy to learn, hard to master is essential for highlighting the individual skills of players. At the moment when a player is making an impossible move, the adoration of the audience depends on their understanding that this move was a masterpiece of skill. The better everybody understands the steep learning curve at the top, the more ecstatically they will cheer on the professional players.

Easy to learn, hard to master as a principle is an underlying assumption on which everything in the eSports industry is built. Understanding this difference helps to attract an audience, as well as highlighting that only a few talented, passionate players will become the very best in the world. Any stakeholder depends on this underlying assumption to attract a big audience and have fierce competition. Following this principle enables all stakeholders to create a thriving business around a certain eSports title. However, the task of creating a title following this principle is not entirely the duty of the video game developer: tournament organizers, professional teams, and players are also necessary to improve any potential title, so it is easy to learn and to watch, and hard to master.

Shifting Metagame

The next governing principle is also rooted in the game design and is one of the most striking changes in game design in recent years, as well as the core difference to traditional sports. Popular eSports titles change constantly, have new content, experience patches, and shift the metagame. Garfield (2013) defines metagame as follows:

A particular game, played with the same rules will mean different things to different people, and those differences are the metagame. The rules of poker may not change between a casino game, a neighborhood nickel-dime-quarter game, and a game played for matchsticks, but the player experience in these games will certainly change. The experience of roleplaying with a group of story-oriented players and playing with some goal-oriented power gamers is entirely different, even though the underlying rules being played with may be the same. There is, of course, no game without a metagame—by this definition. A game without a metagame is like an idealized object in physics. It may be a useful construct, but it doesn't really exist.

The metagame describes the interaction between the player and the game, and this interaction may change over time. The player will continuously look for new ways to play the game and find ways for competitive advantage within the game; however, if the game is continually changing, this process of metagaming will also constantly shift.

Although the metagame metaphor became popular in eSports with *League of Legends* and its ongoing changes, leading to an ever-changing shift (Donaldson 2017), the metagame construct is rooted in game theory and is conceptualized as the metagame analysis (Howard 1971). These shared roots become apparent when looking at the original definition of metagame: "A metagame is the game that would exist if one of the players chose his strategy after the others, in knowledge of their choices" (Howard 1971, p. 23). The metagame analysis is, consequently, utilized as a way to establish potential scenarios for future outcomes: it was applied to military studies in the Cold War (Richelson 1979) and as a way to analyze the Watergate affair (Meleskie et al. 1982).

Furthermore, the metagame analysis is also applied to the business context as a way to identify a competitive strategy linking the metagame to strategic management (Dutta and King 1980) and managerial decision-making (Radford 1975). The metagame analysis was accessible in the 1970s and 1980s because of the rational and mechanical approach; however, other concepts replaced this way of analytical thinking. Still, the metagame paradigm observed in the closed context of a video game has its effects on the eSports industry and how strategic decisions are made.

The metagame assumption, being dynamic, is not an entirely useful assumption for the eSports industry, mainly as it primarily focuses on future scenarios. If the metagame is changing, strategies become obsolete and, more importantly, they become irrelevant as new and innovative strategies are required. This mindset, however, also implies an inherent devaluation of the past, and the past becomes somewhat forgotten. The history is shrouded in a veil of ignorance (Rawls 1971). This historical amnesia is further increased by the game design concept 'fog of war', in which the importance of up-to-date information is highlighted. Historical information is becoming less and less relevant. A focus on the present and the future is useful for innovation, but there is an observable emerging pattern in eSports that many stakeholders in eSports are repeating mistakes of the past.

Furthermore, several stakeholders also neglect the importance of a solid understanding of the business. Although eSports is capable of exploring new ideas and exploiting existing concepts (Scholz and Stein 2017), some are heavily focused on the exploration aspect without exploiting the products, resources, and capabilities that already exist. This development leads to a spiral in which these organizations have to continually find new markets and new investors, a development that is highly risky. The eSports organization OpTic Gaming is expanding massively into new markets such as India, and just recently a player of OpTic was caught cheating (Fogel 2018). Innovation is necessary, but harnessing innovation requires solid strategic management that can exploit the exploration, and this includes a process of learning from the past.

This form of historical amnesia can be seen in various cases, but the most prominent examples are the hypes surrounding the discussion about eSports becoming Olympic and the introduction of geolocated franchises. The relationship with the Olympic Committee especially is an ongoing interaction between two different worlds. In 2018, the International Olympic Committee invited various key people from eSports for discussion with the traditional sports world (Reuters 2018). Two critical demands, however, were an institutionalization of the eSports world, similar to the sports world, and less violent games (Batchelor 2018). Subsequently, the message was follow our rules and you will be legitimated. In the months after that event, several people discussed the need for an Olympic event in eSports, neglecting the long history of the World Cyber Games being an Olympic event in eSports. People were blinded by the potential of being part of the Olympic Games, forgetting their own past and, most importantly, the WCG failed because it could not establish a solid business model. It is questionable if an Olympiad is a substantial investment, albeit the respective countries mostly pay it. A similar situation of historical amnesia can be observed in the context of the current franchise craze in eSports. Although the topic of franchises is nothing new—it existed at the time of the Championship Gaming Series—many stakeholders are praising the creation of geolocation as the new and innovative concept that will change eSports drastically. In a recent report by Goldman Sachs, it is stated as a fact that "by creating geolocated teams, these leagues have opened the door to revenue streams that are unavailable to generalized leagues" (Murray 2018), interestingly neglecting to state that the CGS was also the first geolocated league.

Furthermore, many teams have at least a certain home country, but some teams, like Mousesports, always had a geolocational boundary—in their case, Berlin. Still, many are nowadays normatively creating a reality that geolocation is the future for eSports, but neglecting that this failed before and is counterintuitive to the approach whereby many traditional sports organizations are trying to become an international brand. Many eSports teams have the potential to create a better local brand but, at the same time, they have the potential to become a global brand. Traditional sports organizations may have better ways to access their local revenues, but they are slowly pushing toward an international market. Take the example of Juventus Turin acquiring Cristiano Ronaldo and in 24 hours selling jerseys worth $60 million (Dawson 2018). A small portion of that was probably from Turin; therefore, it seems strange to think that geolocation is the future of eSports.

A compelling case of historical amnesia can be seen in the context of the Battle Royale games. It is often stated that Battle Royale, like *Fortnite*, is a new phenomenon; however, the *Unreal Tournament* in the 2000s had a mode called Deathmatch which was quite similar to the game design idea that there are many players and ultimately one winner. Other games like *Minecraft* had a comparable mode to Battle Royale. Furthermore, the concept of last man standing is not novel for eSports. At the beginning of the millennium, the tournament format 'King of the Hill' was quite popular and consisted of the idea that there is a single king that everybody tries to dethrone. If the king loses a game, the winner becomes the new king. This format was especially popular in *Warcraft III*. Although Battle Royale is an old concept, people do treat games like *Fortnite* as something entirely novel and innovative.

Although this historical amnesia can be dangerous for the business model and, especially, in the context of overheating the market, the positive side is that there is constant change. Notably, where eSports titles are concerned, it is observable that every three to five years a groundbreaking and disruptive game emerges (Hilgers, cited in Ashton 2018) that shakes up the eSports industry. Consequently, absorptive capacity, as the "ability to recognize the value of new information, assimilate it, and apply it to commercial ends" (Cohen and Levinthal 1990, p. 128), is firmly embedded in the eSports industry, and many stakeholders are capable of transforming the knowledge into something useful: they are therefore highly proficient in absorptive capacity and can create competitive advantage out of it. But in a volatile market like eSports, stakeholders need to move fast and not break things, instead creating an environment in which they learn from mistakes and develop efficient processes to turn novel ideas into a profitable business model. Consequently, regarding a shifting metagame, there are the stakeholders that identify innovative areas (potential absorptive capacities) and those that can exploit these capabilities and create a business around these innovations (realized absorptive capacities) (Jansen et al. 2005).

Welcome to the Wild West

It is stated as an ongoing mantra that eSports is like the Wild West, but what does 'Wild West' mean? It is often linked with the new frontier of the US moving West: "America as a wide-open land of unlimited opportunity for the strong, ambitious, self-reliant individual to thrust his way to the top" (Slotkin 1973, p. 5). But was it so wild as to be an ungovernable region with mavericks and bandits? Dykstra (2009) explains the rise of the 'wild' metaphor as especially due to the popular culture of the time (books and stories) and in modern times (movies). However, the scarcity of reliable data was the main reason for the distortion in perception. Especially within a small group, information spreads quickly, and information about adverse events is spread more easily. Furthermore, the government was not yet established, but that does not mean the West was lawless. The Wild West was self-governed and self-organized, creating adequate rules and institutions necessary for this environment (Anderson and Hill 2004).

A similar distortion in perception can be seen in eSports concerning doping. It is known that traditional sports have a doping problem; however, this is not seen as being the 'Wild West'. Some institutions fight against doping, like WADA, though they are losing (Catlin et al. 2008). However, they have media constructed an absolute reality in which eSports also has a doping problem, especially as, until 2015, it had no doping tests or any other way to control doping. Consequently, everybody was shocked when Kory Friesen openly admitted using Adderall and went so far as to claim that everybody is using it. Since then, doping tests have become the norm in professional events, and the ESL announced a list of banned substances in 2015. People could accuse the various stakeholders of having neglected this topic and only reactively created specific regulations. Still, though the scandal led to a fierce reaction to stop a potential doping trend in eSports, the ESL started to perform doping tests at its tournaments in cooperation with an anti-doping agency (Graham 2016). Surprisingly, after 400 tests, mostly in *Counter-Strike*, it seems that eSports are mostly free of doping (Patterson 2018). Still, many media outlets point toward the accusations of Kory Friesen and deduce from this single incident that eSports has a doping problem. It may be the case that there are some black sheep who are doping, but it is not really the Wild West.

It is a fact that eSports has less regulation and less governance than any traditional sport. But are all the rules, all the governance, all the regulations necessary? Liberals would say no, and that is quite striking. In any other industry, less institutionalized regulation is seen as an opportunity: in eSports, it is seen as a disadvantage. However, eSports is not less regulated at all. The game developers, especially Activision Blizzard, are showing that eSports, far from being the Wild West, is enforcing rules and regulations for the games (Partin 2018b). It may be different from the way sports are governed in any other sports industry, but having the power to enforce any command is the opposite of the Wild West metaphor. The Wild West was an ongoing competition, and any form of monopoly was absent until the government stepped in (Billington and Ridge 2001).

Looking at Slotkin's (1973) definition, suddenly the Wild West metaphor seems like a positive thing, even though the media often use it in a negative context. The Wild West was a time when ambitious people could reach the top. That is something we can observe in eSports, where people like Sam Matthews (Fnatic) and Jack Etienne (Cloud9) created their own eSports empires. This freedom is still the main difference from traditional sports, where federations dominate the regulations and enforce their rules. Take a look at the NBA as a franchise league, or the Premier League in Great Britain as a league of teams owned by billionaires. There is no longer any space for any 'Wild West' or for people to create an uproar. The eSports industry, until now, has kept its start-up mentality, and the lack of enforced regulations may lead to a system in which lean management is the preferred approach.

As stated before, being lean and agile is seen in the management literature as an innovative way to utilize dynamic capabilities and to compete proactively in a highly volatile market. Furthermore, the increased competition keeps everybody alert to risks and opportunities. However, many people in eSports are susceptible to outside influences, especially as they suffer from an inferiority complex (Lingle 2016). Consequently, legitimated institutions like sports federations, sports organizations, and television media are seen as important, as their approval is considered necessary for the growth of eSports. At least, this is the observable narrative. The eSports industry is the Wild West and, to become legitimated, it has to adapt to traditional structures and traditional ideals. The strength of the Wild West was that people conquered a new world with new ideas and innovative concepts. Especially in the sports context, many of the traditional institutions do understand that they need to learn from eSports to reach a young audience. Copying the traditional structures and governance from sports and media may be a fatal approach, as traditional sports and media struggle to reach a young audience. The old way does not work to conquer the Wild West, as seen by the disaster of the Championship Gaming Series, and this may happen again with the Overwatch League.

However, the Wild West, as defined by the media, re-emerged in eSports in recent years—not because of the existing primary stakeholders, however, but the secondary stakeholders. These stakeholders are predominantly investors, sports organizations, and sports personalities experiencing an intense fear of missing out. They pump money into the scene, creating a destabilization in the stable competition environment (Lewis 2018). The amount of money has led to a massive rise in salaries. Teams have a sudden influx of cash and have to show their investors some form of growth. This influx of money has led to an actual Wild West situation, but it was created by stakeholders who should understand the importance of a business model and robust organic growth. Several eSports organizations announced layoffs in late 2018, and, although this may be a correction to an overheating market (Cocke 2018), the comment that an organization "grew too fast" (Fischer 2018) is a weak sign of systemic problems. Due to the distortion, eSports organizations are struggling to translate the investor capital into profit. The recent Wild West was externally induced by regulated and institutionalized stakeholders, leading to the conclusion that they do not understand the eSports industry and, consequently, prefer their own structures. But this may be a mistake, as eSports is a collection of competitive gaming, and therefore not governable, as sports in their entirety are not manageable. Embracing this understanding will be faithful to the Wild West as a land of unlimited opportunities.

Born Digital, Born Global, Born Agile

The most relevant and exciting governing principle in eSports is the idea that it is highly digital, genuinely global, and extremely agile. The industry is built upon the shoulders of computerization and the internet. Furthermore, it challenges existing rules and creates products to resolve its needs. Concepts like the LAN party, streaming of the event, and even the idea that there is a market for gaming chairs show that the industry is agile and attentive to change. The stakeholders in eSports were among the first to utilize the digital and global characteristics evolving around the 2000s, both the industry and the stakeholders being born digital, born global, and born agile.

This mindset is highly engrained in the eSports industry, and it is therefore common to have organizations spanning the world with a global staff connected digitally. Many works of literature on today's international virtual teams describe phenomena that have been common in eSports for decades (e.g., Shachaf 2008; van Knippenberg and Mell 2016). There is no border, and there are no barriers: a shared vocabulary can overcome even language difficulties. Being a volatile and fast-paced market is also engrained in the industry, making change a common thing.

But the most exciting aspect of eSports is that it is one of the first industries to have a reverse setting. Many industries started local, analog, and quite stable, and these industries tried to internationalize, digitize, and become more agile. The eSports industry, however, is trying to become more local by creating geolocated leagues and reaching a local audience. It is creating local tournaments in arenas around the world. Finally, the eSports industry is trying to develop some form of stability to make sustainable business growth possible. Everything is in reverse and, consequently, eSports is unique in its settings. The eSports industry, like everybody else, is trying to balance analog and digital, local and global, and stability and agility, but it has mastered digitization, globalization, and agility already. It will be difficult to achieve the other aspects without neglecting the crucial competitive advantage of already being digital, global, and agile.

References

Ashton, Graham. 2018. RSR Partners x HIVE New York: Full Day Recap. Accessed 2 November 2018. https://esportsobserver.com/rsr-partners-x-hive-new-york-full-day-recap.

Anderson, Terry L., and Peter J. Hill. 2004. *The Not So Wild, Wild West: Property Rights on the Frontier*. Stanford, CA: Stanford University Press.

Batchelor, James. 2018. No Esports in Olympics Because 'Killer Games' Promote Violence. Accessed 2 November 2018. https://www.gamesindustry.biz/

articles/2018-09-04-no-esports-in-olympics-because-killer-games-promote-violent.

Berger, Peter L., and Thomas Luckmann. 1966. *The Social Construction of Reality: A Treatise in the Sociology of Knowledge*. New York: Anchor Books.

Billington, Ray A., and Martin Ridge. 2001. *Westward Expansion: A History of the American Frontier*. Albuquerque: University of New Mexico Press.

Bogost, Ian. 2009. Persuasive Games: Familiarity, Habituation, and Catchiness. Accessed 2 November 2018. http://www.gamasutra.com/view/feature/3977/persuasive_games_familiarity_.php.

Catlin, D.H., K.D. Fitch, and A. Ljungqvist. 2008. Medicine and Science in the Fight Against Doping in Sport. *Journal of Internal Medicine* 264 (2): 99–114.

Cifaldi, Frank. 2010. GDC: Blizzard's Core Game Design Concepts. Accessed 2 November 2018. http://www.gamasutra.com/view/news/27640/GDC_Blizzards_Core_Game_Design_Concepts.php.

Cocke, Taylor. 2018. Cuts at Infinite Esports and Echo Fox Signal an Esports Correction, Not Trouble. Accessed 2 November 2018. https://esportsobserver.com/infinite-esports-echo-fox-cuts.

Cohen, Wesley M., and Daniel A. Levinthal. 1990. Absorptive Capacity: New Perspectives on Learning and Innovation. *Administrative Science Quarterly* 35 (1): 128–152.

Dawson, Alan. 2018. Juventus Reportedly Sold $60 Million Worth of Ronaldo Jerseys in 24 Hours—Almost Half His Transfer Fee. Accessed 2 November 2018. https://www.businessinsider.de/juventus-sold-60-million-in-cristiano-ronaldo-jerseys-in-24-hours-2018-7?r=US&IR=T.

Donaldson, Scott. 2017. Mechanics and Metagame: Exploring Binary Expertise in League of Legends. *Games and Culture* 12 (5): 426–444.

Dutta, Biplab K., and William R. King. 1980. Metagame Analysis of Competitive Strategy. *Strategic Management Journal* 1 (4): 357–370.

Dykstra, Robert R. 2009. Quantifying the Wild West: The Problematic Statistics of Frontier Violence. *Western Historical Quarterly* 40 (3): 321–347.

Fischer, Ben. 2018. Infinite Esports Cuts Staff, Including President Chris Chaney. Accessed 2 November 2018. https://esportsobserver.com/infinite-esports-cuts-staff.

Fogel, Stefanie. 2018. Pro 'CS_GO' Player 'Forsaken' Receives Five-Year Ban for Cheating. Accessed 2 November 2018. https://variety.com/2018/gaming/news/counter-strike-forsaken-cheating-ban-1202998388.

Garfield, Richard. 2013. Metagames. Accessed 2 November 2018. https://edt-210gamestechsociety.files.wordpress.com/2013/09/2000-garfield-metagame.pdf.

Graham, Roy. 2016. Does Esports Have a Drug Problem. Accessed 2 November 2018. https://killscreen.com/articles/does-esports-have-a-drug-problem.

Howard, Nigel. 1971. *Paradoxes of Rationality: Theory of Metagames and Political Behaviour.* Cambridge, MA: MIT Press.

Jansen, Justin J., Frans A.J. Van Den Bosch, and Henk W. Volberda. 2005. Managing Potential and Realized Absorptive Capacity: How Do Organizational Antecedents Matter? *Academy of Management Journal* 48 (6): 999–1015.

Lewis, Richard. 2018. Richard Lewis at the ESIC, 'Money Flooding into Sports Has, Naturally, Brought With It Corruption at All Levels. Accessed 2 November 2018. https://www.vpesports.com/more-esports/richard-lewis-at-the-esic-money-flooding-into-sports-has-naturally-brought-with-it-corruption-at-all-levels.

Lingle, Samuel. 2016. The Complicated Past (and Future) of Esports on TV. Accessed 2 November 2018. https://kernelmag.dailydot.com/issue-sections/headline-story/16083/eleague-esports-tv-history.

Meleskie, Michael F., Keith W. Hipel, and Niall M. Fraser. 1982. The Watergate Tapes Conflict: A Metagame Analysis. *Political Methodology* 8 (4): 1–23.

Murray, Trent. 2018. Goldman Sachs Esports Report: Esports Revenue to Grow to $2.96B by 2022. Accessed 2 November 2018. https://esportsobserver.com/goldman-sachs-esports-report.

Partin, Will. 2018a. 'StarCraft II': How Blizzard Brought the King of Esports Back From the Dead. Accessed 2 November 2018. https://variety.com/2018/gaming/features/StarCraft-ii-esports-history-1202873246.

———. 2018b. Blizzard's Ban on Third-Party Overwatch Apps was Never About Competitive Integrity. Accessed 2 November 2018. https://variety.com/2018/gaming/columns/blizzards-ban-on-third-party-overwatch-apps-was-never-about-competitive-integrity-1202961745.

Patterson, Calum. 2018. Behind the Scenes Doping Control at CS: GO Event Reveals Surprising Truth About Doping in Esports. Accessed 2 November 2018. https://www.dexerto.com/esports/behind-the-scenes-doping-control-at-csgo-event-reveals-surprising-truth-about-doping-in-esports-137521.

Radford, K.J. 1975. Applications of Metagame Theory in Managerial Decision Making. *Omega* 3 (3): 303–312.

Rawls, John. 1971. *A Theory of Justice.* Cambridge, MA: Harvard University Press.

Reuters. 2018. Esports Players, Leaders to Attend IOC Forum. Accessed 2 November 2018. https://www.reuters.com/article/us-esports-gaming-olympics/esports-players-leaders-to-attend-ioc-forum-idUSKBN1KB0NX.

Richelson, Jeffrey T. 1979. Soviet Strategic Doctrine and Limited Nuclear Operations: A Metagame Analysis. *Journal of Conflict Resolution* 23 (2): 326–336.

Schein, Edgar H. 1985. *Organizational Culture and Leadership. A Dynamic View*. San Francisco, CA: Jossey-Bass.

Scholz, Tobias M., and Volker Stein. 2017. Going Beyond Ambidexterity in the Media Industry: eSports as Pioneer of Ultradexterity. *International Journal of Gaming and Computer-Mediated Simulations* 9 (2): 47–62.

Shachaf, Pnina. 2008. Cultural Diversity and Information and Communication Technology Impacts on Global Virtual Teams: An Exploratory Study. *Information & Management* 45 (2): 131–142.

Slotkin, Richard. 1973. *Regeneration Through Violence: The Mythology of the American Frontier, 1600–1860*. Middleton, CT: Wesleyan University Press.

van Knippenberg, Daan, and Julija N. Mell. 2016. Past, Present, and Potential Future of Team Diversity Research: From Compositional Diversity to Emergent Diversity. *Organizational Behavior and Human Decision Processes* 136: 135–145.

WoWProgress. 2018. Mythic Progress. Accessed 2 November 2018. http://www.wowprogress.com.

5

The Business Model Network

Abstract The eSports industry is highly volatile and in the midst of exponential growth; however, it becomes evident that a common understanding influences the eSports industry. The focus is on a value integration toward the audience and doing business around this audience. Furthermore, there are three existing rules: coopetition, co-destiny, and convergence. These rules imply an increased interconnectedness of stakeholders and result in a tight business model network. However, with the entrance of new organizations, the business model network may experience frictions and this development may in the future lead to changes in the business model network of the eSports industry, eventually changing the prevailing rules of coopetition, co-destiny, and convergence.

Keywords eSports • Business model network • Coopetition • Co-destiny • Convergence

© The Author(s) 2019
T. M. Scholz, *eSports is Business*, https://doi.org/10.1007/978-3-030-11199-1_5

Going Beyond Five Forces to Focus on Value Integration

The eSports industry with its various stakeholders can be seen as an interwoven network, where stakeholders need each other to work and to succeed. Although eSports organizations challenge existing business models, they are part of the value creation. However, the chance to emerge untouched for an extended period without the strong interaction of traditional industries may have led to an evolution that is different from existing industries. The eSports industry is driven by innovations and technologies, but also by the interconnection of creative people trying to exploit technologies to the fullest. Technology has always been a driver for change rather than a barrier to conquer; however, this strong momentum, pushing the limits, created an environment in which preexisting business models could not be used for eSports, and it had to find its own way to build a business, sometimes in an environment where an organization did not know that a specific area of its work could become a thriving business model. Take the example of Twitch being a spin-off of Justin.tv, only to grow into the driving business for this company and eventually being sold to Amazon. This unique setting, aligned with the start-up mentality and an understanding of interconnectedness, led to a distinct network of stakeholders. Although the eSports industry is continuously evolving, the knowledge of being a network eventually to monetize the audience is still a driving force of every business model in the eSports industry, as depicted in Fig. 5.1.

This increased interconnection underlines the importance of a business model network in which the business models of every stakeholder interact with the other business models, leading to an increase in profitability throughout the system. The business model network thereby goes beyond the understanding of value creation based on the five forces defined by Porter (1985). The business model network focuses on value integration with an emphasis on cooperation rather than threat. There are threats of new entries, buyer power, and supplier power, a risk of substitution, and competitive rivalry, but there is also a need for cooperation to utilize syner-

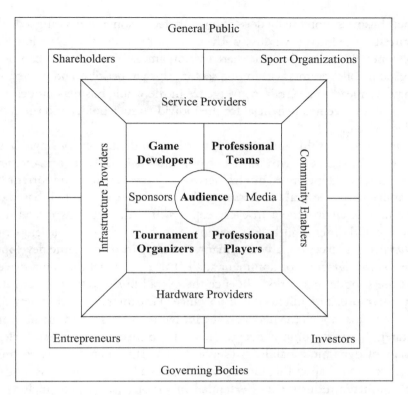

Fig. 5.1 Ongoing evolution of the stakeholder network, highlighting the importance of the business model network

gies. And, contrary to the five forces, there is also a certain synergy that allows strategic management, connecting the business models. This network simultaneously relies on cooperation and competition, this coopetition (Brandenburger and Nalebuff 1996) highlighting the potential to improve the whole network by cooperating in certain areas and fiercely competing in others. Even if organizations are competitors in a specific market, they may collaborate in a different market if they complement one another. There is a strategic benefit for the organization to assist a competitor. Based on that premise of strategic orientation, coopetition can go beyond the mere coordination of services from a profitability perspective. As competitors collaborate, they can discover a shared understanding of their business, potentially developing a shared vision and devising a deliberate strategy for their industry. The concept of co-destiny (Davidow and Malone 1992) describes this shared vision among a network of competitors and collaborators within one sector. This coopetition and co-destiny may even lead to a certain convergence in the whole business model network if it is deemed beneficial for the individual stakeholder and the complete system.

Focusing on value integration toward the audience, every single business model is linked with other business models in the network, creating one combined business model network. However, it is important to emphasize that several business model networks are connected. Based on the unique environment in every eSports title, the business model network could differ slightly. For example, the role of the game developer in *Overwatch* is exceptionally dominant, but the part of the game developer in *Counter-Strike* is not dominant at all. This means that the game-driven business model networks influence the overall business model network. Furthermore, it highlights the importance of the interconnection between the business model, the network, the individual strategy, and the network strategy in a dynamic concept. This interconnection requires efficient usage of dynamic capabilities (Teece 2018). This chapter is based on a forthcoming chapter (Scholz forthcoming) in a book on business models in the media industry: it is extended in various aspects and includes a discussion of potential convergent moves in the eSports industry.

Three Cs as Simple Rules

Coopetition

Coopetition is one of the driving forces in the eSports industry, and many stakeholders, especially veterans, follow the rules of coopetition. While competition is crucial for the survival of any eSports organization, it cannot be achieved without some level of collaboration. Mutual recognition of interdependence is a precondition for coopetition and, especially in eSports, it becomes evident that a game developer may require tournament organizers but depends on professional teams and professional players. Walley (2007,

p. 11) describes coopetition, based on Bengtsson and Kock (2003), as "a situation where competitors simultaneously cooperate and compete with each other". This concept marks a shift from the traditional view that inter-firm dynamics have to be either competitive or cooperative. Coopetition gained popularity through Brandenburger and Nalebuff (1996), who, in their seminal work, used game theory to prove the potential benefits of cooperation in a competitive market. Value creation may foster competition, as companies compete for customers or suppliers, but value creation is also linked to a value network in which everybody can learn from each other. This form of cooperation can foster knowledge (Tsai 2002), creativity (Brolos 2009), and innovation (Gnyawali and Park 2011). It may be beneficial for any organization to utilize cooperation, even with competitors. Although coopetition may be a driving force in the eSports industry, we can observe similar coopetitive relationships in other industries. For example, Apple and Samsung are main competitors, but Samsung is also one of the leading suppliers for Apple. They compete and cooperate at the same time.

Coopetition is an essential cornerstone of the eSports industry and has helped to create novel and innovative ideas. Some eSports stakeholders compete fiercely against each other in terms of reaching the audience, but, at the same time, they cooperate to foster growth. There is a certain observable tendency toward cocreation (Brenda 2017). All companies learn from each other to create a better and, consequently, more profitable product. Examples like the problematic relationship between Activision Blizzard and KeSPA concerning *StarCraft* in South Korea showed a form of coopetition: both stakeholders wanted to foster the growth of *StarCraft* in South Korea and, although they may struggle with each other, *StarCraft* grew exponentially in that country and solidified the claim of that country being the powerhouse of eSports. The competitive and cooperative relationship led to the domination of Korean *StarCraft* players for nearly two decades and may have fostered the recent Korean domination in *Overwatch*.

Co-destiny

Coopetition may be helpful for stakeholders to understand the benefits of cooperating with other stakeholders, but the primary goal is to create a business model that helps the stakeholder to grow and profit. If there is a benefit in cooperating, every organization will collaborate. Cooperation may be especially intriguing in an emerging and growing industry, as long as there is some profit in it, but cooperation may vanish immediately if this profit is gone. The rules of competition mainly drive coopetition.

The eSports industry has for decades shown a particular behavior wherein a specific shared vision or co-destiny is observable. This shared vision is especially important for the co-destiny process (Davidow and Malone 1992; Scholz 2000). Several eSports stakeholders share a long-term goal and strategy for seeing eSports grow. That vision will even come with short-term sacrifices to create growth that ultimately helps every stakeholder. Usually, this shared understanding is governed by some institution, like an association or federation. These institutions will have the power to enforce specific regulations that may be harmful in the short term but can be helpful for long-term growth. eSports has no governing body and no institutions big enough to create a shared vision, but eSports is strongly driven by a certain co-destiny. Many people involved in eSports love eSports, and they want to see eSports grow. This co-destiny is especially shared with long-term stakeholders, but even younger stakeholders seem to adopt this co-destiny (e.g., Rick Fox, former basketball player and owner of Echo Fox).

One crucial requirement for co-destiny, however, is trust between individual eSports companies. Despite fierce competition, a certain degree of confidence prevails. This trust has evolved and originates from the industry's tit-for-tat sentiment. Especially in the beginning, eSports were sometimes comparable to the Wild West: there were no rules, and there were no business experts. Everything was based on the principle of trial and error. Those whose actions promoted their interest at the expense of eSports as a whole, however, were isolated. Consequently, eSports features a trust network alongside an informal code of conduct. There are actual governing rules and principles, and there is an understanding and shared vision of eSports. This may change as companies from outside eSports (e.g., sports and media companies) become more deeply involved.

Convergence

Based on the underlying rules of coopetition and co-destiny, it can be stated that there is also a particular rule in the tendency toward convergence in the eSports industry. However, the form of convergence is not precise for the industry, especially as the audience is the primary target and the goal is to increase growth. However, that means that there is a specific drive toward convergence of successful concepts and ideas. Converging trends are often discussed in the context of neo-institutionalism (DiMaggio and Powell 1983) and the tendency of organizations to become similar over time (Beckert 2010). Where the eSports industry is concerned, a tendency toward sigma-convergence may be hypothesized, meaning that the variance between eSports organizations becomes less with time (Heichel et al. 2005).

This sigma-convergence is relevant, because if eSports stakeholders do share coopetition and co-destiny, they will become similar over time. New stakeholders may introduce changes and new developments, or eSports titles may disrupt the industry, and there will be a diffusion of those ideas, but over time a specific form of convergence is observable (Rogers 1962). The extreme disruption introduced by the Championship Gaming Series may have led to short-term divergence, but, in the end, it contributed to an overall convergence in the industry. This convergence toward a thriving eSports industry that enables individual stakeholders to thrive may be a clear rule that contributed to the recent exponential growth. However, it also led to a massive spike in newcomers on the scene, resulting in another divergence in the scene by introducing a variety of divergent forces.

In summary, eSports companies compete intensely within the boundaries of their network while at the same time benefitting greatly from cooperation. Still, eSports companies go beyond the traditional understanding of coopetition. Therefore, boosting eSports altogether is a common goal for every member of this network. This mutual goal increases the survivability of the network as a whole, and that of every single one of its members, especially given the strong interconnection between actors. Co-destiny has led to more trust in the entire business model network, especially as the customer is the heart of any eSports company.

124   T. M. Scholz

Value Integration in the Business Model Network

In recent years, the concept of business models has received significant attention (Klang et al. 2014). Despite the significance of the term for strategic management (Zott et al. 2011), there is no shared consensus on the use of this term in the business context (e.g., DaSilva and Trkman 2014). The number of critics of the concept is high, a prominent one being Porter (2001, p. 73): "The definition of business model is murky at best. Most often, it seems to refer to a loose conception of how a company does business and generates revenue". Still, the general idea of a business model is useful for creating a sustainable business (Foss and Saebi 2017), establishing a "design or architecture of the value creating, delivery, and capture mechanisms" (Teece 2010, p. 172). The importance of the business model, therefore, is to create value and translate value into revenue. To categorize the process of business model creation strategically, Chesbrough and Rosenbloom (2002, p. 533–534) derived the following functions of a business model:

- Articulate the value proposition, i.e. the value created for users by the offering based on the technology.
- Identify a market segment, i.e. the users to whom the technology is useful and for what purpose, and specify the revenue generation mechanism(s) for the firm.
- Define the structure of the value chain within the firm required to create and distribute the offering, and determine the complementary assets needed to support the firm's position in this chain.
- Estimate the cost structure and profit potential of producing the offering, given the value proposition and value chain structure chosen.
- Describe the position of the firm within the value network, linking suppliers and customers, including identification of potential complementors and competitors.
- Formulate the competitive strategy by which the innovating firm will gain and hold advantage over rivals.

Although the business model is the core of any business, the term only gained popularity in the 1990s, despite being mentioned for the first time in 1957 (Bellman et al. 1957). The current narrative links the business model with the strategic management and states that the business model has a short-term focus but is interconnected with the strategy. Consequently, a business model needs a plan and a strategy needs a business model (DaSilva and Trkman 2014), at least for a professional and successful organization. Therefore, the statement "every organization has some business model" and "not every organization has a strategy" (Casadesus-Masanell and Ricart 2010, p. 206) seems fitting.

Furthermore, the business model can be dynamic and shift from time to time as appropriate to the general strategy: therefore a business model can be compared to "a process that deliberately changes the core elements of a firm and its business logic" (Bucherer et al. 2012, p. 184). Yunus et al. (2010, p. 312) highlight that "business model innovation is about generating new sources of profit by finding novel value proposition/value constellation combinations". Khanagha et al. (2014, p. 325) identify the following goals for business model innovation: "aligning internal activities with the external rate and direction of change", "retaining resources and capabilities", and "minimizing the costs of change".

The business model and the business model innovation depend on the network surrounding the organization (Zott and Amit 2009); therefore, every business model is intertwined with the business model of others in its network. Although this interconnectedness may not influence the strategy, the business model will be affected and will impact other business models. Molded by coopetition, co-destiny, and convergent forces, the eSports industry has a highly interconnected business model network. The business model network was for a long time isolated from external influences; however, in recent years, new forces have joined the market. These include entrepreneurs, media businesses, sports organizations, and investors looking for ways to profit from the exponential growth of eSports. This development of different stakeholders joining the eSports industry has led to some friction in the established and isolated business model network. The strategic background of these newcomers can be varied and, at least initially, will disturb the business model network. Whether this friction is dissolved depends on the coopetition, co-destiny, and convergence of the existing eSports stakeholders. Still, the primary goal of any of these organizations is to create value, and it is therefore necessary to follow the value integration as the audience is, for all stakeholders, the core of the business. For this transition period, it is possible to categorize companies as follows according to their strategic orientations and their effect on their business models.

- 'Traditional' eSports organizations with extensive knowledge of the eSports industry have business models organized around a strong belief in a co-destiny shared with other participants in the eSports media realm.
- Entrepreneurs with prior experience in other industries and markets have business models focused on the innovation value of their products and the profits these products can generate.
- Media businesses are likely to see eSports as a media business and bring to it business models focused on exploiting perceived synergies with their existing media services.
- Sports organizations based in more traditional offline sports have business models focused on integrating eSports into their current portfolios of sports properties and employing tactics that worked there to increase their eSports properties' audiences and fan bases.
- Investors have business models focused on capitalizing on the current growth and projected growth for eSports.

All of these strategic orientations influence the business model and how newcomers will enter the eSports industry, resulting in an initial clash. Every business model will have an impact on the eSports industry, challenging the coopetition, co-destiny, and convergence, potentially transforming the eSports industry, or transforming the strategic orientation of the newcomers. Table 5.1 gives an overview of the business model influenced by newcomers' distinct background and how stakeholders may interact.

The value proposition in the various business model orientations shows a focus on knowledge of eSports (eSports-driven), expertise in professional media (media-driven), or expertise in creating a sports experience (sports-driven). These various driving forces also highlight friction in the potential value chain of a business model network, as the media-driven and sports-

Table 5.1 The key business model attributes of the different categorizations (Scholz forthcoming)

	Value proposition	Value chain	Cost and profit	Value network	Competitive strategy	Coopetition/co-destiny
eSports-driven	Enthusiastic eSports experience	Based on the existing eSports value chain	Modest profit in order to achieve sustainability	Embedded in the network and knowledge	"Gaming is believing"	Understands the co-destiny and eSports tradition
Entrepreneur-driven	Innovation and change through technology	Adapting to the existing eSports value chain	High cost at the beginning, hope for profit in the far future	Acting as outsider searching for a place in the network	Be innovative and jump on the bandwagon	Coopetition as long as necessary but no co-destiny
Media-driven	Professional media coverage	Integration into existing media value chain	Moderate and fearful investment	Acting as outsider searching for a place in the network	Better media coverage based on experience	Understands the need for coopetition and co-destiny
Sports-driven	Professional and traditional sports experience	Integration into existing sports value chain	High initial cost, profit seemingly irrelevant	Acting as outsider, mostly ignoring existing network	Supplying experience on how to organize sports	Focus on competition as practiced in sports
Investor-driven	Supplying capital for growth	Adapting to the existing eSports value chain	High initial cost, profit in the near future	Acting as outsider, buying into the existing network	Winner takes it all	Cooperation is only relevant if essential for profit

driven business models want to integrate their business model in eSports into the existing business model in their respective areas of business. Investors and entrepreneurs are more open to adapting to the current value chain; however, they have specific ideas of how that may look. Where cost and profit are concerned, the potential disruption is also observable, especially in relation to entrepreneurs, investors, and sports organizations, as they invest heavily in eSports. Whereas entrepreneurs and investors want to see a profit, sports organizations seem to invest to be part of the eSports industry. Both strategies challenge the existing strategy of eSports organizations and media businesses, potentially being highly destabilizing, as the market is flooded with money and only some will ask for a return on investment. It becomes essential to understand that these newcomers will have to seek their place in the value network to participate in the value integration toward monetization of the audience. There is a tendency to try to integrate themselves into the existing eSports business model network (entrepreneur-driven, media-driven, and investor-driven). However, sports-driven business models currently ignore the existing network and will need to address this friction in the future, especially as they want to connect access to a young audience with their business of being a traditional sports organization. Finally, the competitive strategy is vastly different for all orientations. The eSports-driven business models focus on the shared dream of eSports and their passion; the entrepreneur-driven business models focus on their innovativeness; media-driven companies present their experience in media coverage; sports-driven teams are better in relation to organized sports; and the competitive strategy of an investor-driven business model is that, in the end, the winner will grab everything.

The rules of coopetition, co-destiny, and convergence were created in the eSports industry by existing organizations, and newcomers will have to find a way to deal with these rules to find their place in the business model network. It may be the case that the rules will change in the future; however, newcomers have to address these rules now. Some examples already show that newcomers are adapting, as seen with Rick Fox as one of the earliest investors with a traditional sports background. Other cases show that an existing eSports organization like Activision Blizzard could enforce convergence for a distinct league through a rigid franchise system.

In many cases, convergence of media-driven newcomers is observable; however, they already had a long history in eSports. In the early 2000s, they tried to enforce their business model and failed to transfer it to eSports. Today, the media businesses understand their role in the business model network and contribute to the eSports industry. For example, NBC or ESPN are trying to improve the production value, or the story-telling, of competition. ESPN is becoming a part of the eSports business model network and did not try to transform, but rather improved the system in alignment with the co-destiny. Still, it is essential for the stake-holders to find their role in the business model network to contribute to the value integration toward the audience. Without a contributing role in the business model network, they will struggle to make a profit in both the short and the long term.

Cases of Different Developments Based on the Various Driving Forces

The business model network will still be the driving force for the growth of eSports and of individual stakeholders in the future; however, its evolution is unclear. The most powerful stakeholder will shape the future of the eSports industry, despite it being questionable who the most influential stakeholder is. At the moment, many would say that the game developers owning the intellectual property of the game are the most probable driving force, but even that is debatable, as there is an observable plateauing. The eSports market does not seem to be growing for all eternity, but can experience a level of saturation. For example, The International in *Dota 2* seems to be growing slowly out-side China (ESC.watch 2018), and a similar phenomenon can be observed in many other eSports titles. This means that game developers may have to deal with competition and can no longer comfortably enforce their intellectual property rights. It may even be the case that they anticipate this development, creating franchises to bind profes-sional teams to their game and lock them into their business model network. However, the recent development of various Battle Royale games shows that game developers are losing power. Figure 5.2 depicts

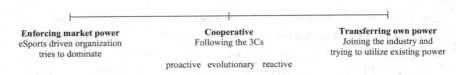

Fig. 5.2 Potential developments for the future evolution of business model networks

ways in which the business model network could be influenced in the future, with the potential choice of foster divergence or convergence.

Enforcing market power can be observed with Activision Blizzard and the creation of the franchise league *Overwatch*, as well as the rumored franchising of *Call of Duty* and the offering of a spot to the existing franchise owner in *Overwatch*. Recent developments in *Hearthstone* also hint at centralization in this game. *Heroes of the Storm* is kept alive by the game developer, and Activision Blizzard heavily influences most of the tournaments. Concerning *StarCraft*, the game was nearly killed in the effort to recapture the IP. Not realizing the success of *StarCraft* in South Korea led to an industry without the game developer, and the game developer tried to win back South Korea by creating *StarCraft II*. Furthermore, at the beginning of *StarCraft II*, many different tournaments were created, leading to uncontrolled growth. Activision Blizzard lost control of its game and IP, so it enforced its power, and today's *StarCraft* scene has dwindled, causing the game stuck to be in a niche. Although the track record of this game developer is not positive regarding creating an eSports league, it has the power to enforce its rules and its environment. The Overwatch League is proof of this power. If the business model and strategy are successful, it will have a sustainable business model with teams, players, and sponsors locked into its business model network, creating a sustainable profit for Activision Blizzard. At the moment, the future of the Overwatch League is not bright, and there is still a risk that the league will collapse in two years with renegotiations concerning media rights and sponsor deals. By enforcing and dominating its business model network, the game developers may diverge from the eSports industry in creating their closed industry and trying to retain every stakeholder.

Another divergent force could be an outside force that is strong enough to disrupt the industry. This may be the Olympic Committee realizing that it needs eSports to stay relevant. The first steps in that direction can already be observed in 2018, when the committee stipulated demands that the eSports industry should follow, especially by creating an international governing body, national federations, and no violence in games. These demands are nearly impossible to enforce and would hypothetically lead to a divergence in eSports—that is, eSports titles that are legitimated by the Olympic Committee and therefore deemed adequate, and other eSports titles that are considered to be inappropriate. Consequently, eSports titles like FIFA would be supported and games like *Counter-Strike* outlawed, resulting in a divergence in the eSports industry. There is the legitimate and therefore right way to create a business in the eSports industry, and there is the illegitimate and wrong way. The way the Olympic Committee is currently arguing would eventually mean a split in the eSports industry, with parts bowing to the traditional governance structures of traditional sports and other parts following the business-driven approach of the current evolution of the eSports industry.

However, neither approach will shape the business model network of the eSports industry in its entirety, but could instead lead to isolated industries for clear titles and may contribute to a fragmentation in the eSports industry. A more likely development is a more cooperative approach in which coopetition, co-destiny, and convergence will continue to be the effective rules for the eSports industry. This collaborative approach can be categorized into a proactive, an evolutionary, and a reactive strategy. The proactive approach actively tries to create coopetition, co-destiny, and convergence, something that can be observed in organizations that seek to foster growth and maturity in eSports. For example, the AnyKey Organization working for a fair and inclusive future in gaming is supported by long-time eSports stakeholders Intel and ESL. They actively seek a way to make the eSports industry grow and change. Concerning evolutionary cooperation, the game developer Valve is a prominent example: although it focuses on a laissez-faire strategy, it tries to enable evolution in its games. Primarily, the game *Counter-Strike* has evolved drastically over the years: Valve has supported these changes and enabled any eSports stakeholder to shape the way *Counter-Strike* is played competitively. This evolutionary approach may not result in a perfect power balance, but *Counter-Strike* is the longest running eSports title (in various evolutions), attracting a big audience for the various tournaments. Finally, the cooperative reactive approach is observable in South Korea and the strategic shift of KeSPA and OGN. After years of staying inside the borders and the downfall of the eSports industry, KeSPA is trying to become a haven for talent. It seeks to create an infrastructure to foster professional players and trainers and export them to the world, something that led to a Korean dominance in *Overwatch*. Furthermore, OGN started trying to distribute its capabilities, creating tournaments by expanding to North America and organizing the *PUBG* league for North America (Pei 2018). It tries to cooperate with the business model network, but only reactively, and by harnessing its existing infrastructure and human capital.

The business model network will change in the coming years, and it may evolve into something entirely new. There is a massive influx of new stakeholders and an enormous increase in capital, potentially creating a new bubble; but, in the long run, the cooperative approach will lead to steady growth in the future. It is evident, especially in hype times, that short-time success may be lucrative, but creating a sustainable business model will trump such short-sighted views. The eSports industry will grow, but mainly because of increasing fragmentation. More eSports titles will be popular, more professional teams will emerge, many professional players will become popular, and so on. Coopetition, co-destiny, and convergence will help to create a business model network in which everybody can contribute to the value integration toward the audience, that way maybe building an industry that is more organized and self-governed compared to the sports industry. However, the current form of business model network is dominated by a convergent trend, highlighting the interconnectedness of all stakeholders trying to create a suitable business model to monetize the growing eSports audience.

References

Beckert, Jens. 2010. Institutional Isomorphism Revisited: Convergence and Divergence in Institutional Change. *Sociological Theory* 28 (2): 150–166.

Bellman, Richard, Charles E. Clark, Donald G. Malcolm, Clifford J. Craft, and Franc M. Ricciardi. 1957. On the Construction of a Multi-Stage, Multi-Person Business Game. *Operations Research* 5 (4): 469–503.

Bengtsson, Maria, and Sören Kock. 2003. Tension in Co-opetition. Paper presented at the Academy of Marketing Science Annual Conference, Washington, DC.

Brandenburger, A.M., and B.J. Nalebuff. 1996. *Co-opetition*. New York: Doubleday.

Brenda, Ho Kai Sze. 2017. Spectating the Rift: A Study into eSports Spectatorship. In *eSports Yearbook 2015/16*, ed. Julia Hiltscher and Tobias M. Scholz, 9–35. Norderstedt, Germany: Books on Demand.

Brolos, Anette. 2009. Innovative Coopetition: The Strength of Strong Ties. *International Journal of Entrepreneurship and Small Business* 8 (1): 110–134.

Bucherer, Eva, Uli Eisert, and Oliver Gassmann. 2012. Towards Systematic Business Model Innovation: Lessons from Product Innovation Management. *Creativity and Innovation Management* 21 (2): 183–198.

Casadesus-Masanell, Ramon, and Joan E. Ricart. 2010. From Strategy to Business Models and Onto Tactics. *Long Range Planning* 43 (2): 195–215.

Chesbrough, Henry, and Richard S. Rosenbloom. 2002. The Role of the Business Model in Capturing Value from Innovation: Evidence from Xerox Corporation's Technology Spin-Off Companies. *Industrial and Corporate Change* 11 (3): 529–555.

DaSilva, Carlos M., and Peter Trkman. 2014. Business Model: What It Is and What It Is Not. *Long Range Planning* 47 (6): 379–389.

Davidow, William H., and Michael S. Malone. 1992. *The Virtual Corporation: Structuring and Revitalizing the Corporation of the 21st Century*. New York: HarperCollins.

DiMaggio, Paul J., and Walter W. Powell. 1983. The Iron Cage Revisited: Institutional Isomorphism and Collective Rationality in Organizational Fields. *American Socio-logical Review* 48 (2): 147–160.

ESC.watch. 2018. The International 2018 Statistics. Accessed 2 November 2018. https://esc.watch/blog/post/stats-international-2018.

Foss, Nicolai J., and Tina Saebi. 2017. Fifteen Years of Research on Business Model Innovation. How Far Have We Come, and Where Should We Go? *Journal of Management* 43 (1): 200–227.

Gnyawali, Devi R., and Byung-Jin R. Park. 2011. Co-opetition Between Giants: Collaboration with Competitors for Technological Innovation. *Research Policy* 40 (5): 650–663.

Heichel, Stephan, Jessica Pape, and Thomas Sommerer. 2005. Is There Convergence in Convergence Research? An Overview of Empirical Studies on Policy Convergence. *Journal of European Public Policy* 12 (5): 817–840.

Khanagha, Saeed, Henk Volberda, and Ilan Oshri. 2014. Business Model Renewal and Ambidexterity: Structural Alteration and Strategy Formation

Process During Transition to a Cloud Business Model. *R&D Management* 44 (3): 322–340.

Klang, David, Maria Wallnöfer, and Fredrik Hacklin. 2014. The Business Model Paradox: A Systematic Review and Exploration of Antecedents. *International Journal of Management Reviews* 16 (4): 454–478.

Pei, Annie. 2018. South Korea Esports Network OGN to Invest at Least $100 Million in North America, Plans Big Partnership with Battle Royale Giant PUBG. Accessed 2 November 2018. https://www.cnbc.com/2018/10/10/esports-network-ogn-to-invest-at-least-100-million-in-north-america.html.

Porter, Michael E. 1985. *Competitive Advantage: Creating and Sustaining Superior Performance*. New York: Simon and Schuster.

———. 2001. Strategy and the Internet. *Harvard Business Review* 79 (3): 62–78.

Rogers, Everett M. 1962. *Diffusion of Innovations*. New York: Free Press of Glencoe.

Scholz, Christian. 2000. *Strategische Organisation. Multiperspektivität und Virtualität*. Landsberg, Lech: moderne industrie.

Scholz, Tobias M. forthcoming. Coopetition and Co-destiny as Business Model: Lessons from the eSports Industry. In *Media Business Models: Connecting Media to Their Markets*, ed. Christian Scholz and Steve Wildman. Porto: Media XXI.

Teece, David J. 2010. Business Models, Business Strategy and Innovation. *Long Range Planning* 43 (2): 172–194.

———. 2018. Business Models and Dynamic Capabilities. *Long Range Planning* 51 (1): 40–49.

Tsai, Wenpin. 2002. Social Structure of 'Coopetition' Within a Multiunit Organization: Coordination, Competition, and Intraorganizational Knowledge Sharing. *Organization Science* 13 (2): 179–190.

Walley, Keith. 2007. Coopetition: An Introduction to the Subject and an Agenda for Research. *International Studies of Management & Organization* 37 (2): 11–31.

Yunus, Muhammad, Bertrand Moingeon, and Laurence Lehmann-Ortega. 2010. Building Social Business Models: Lessons from the Grameen Experience. *Long Range Planning* 43 (2): 308–325.

Zott, Christoph, and Raphael Amit. 2009. The Business Model as the Engine of Network-Based Strategies. In *The Network Challenge. Strategy Profit, and Risk in an Interlinked World*, ed. Paul R. Kleindorfer and Yoram J. Wind, 259–275. Upper Saddle River, NJ: Wharton School Publishing.

Zott, Christoph, Raphael Amit, and Lorenzo Massa. 2011. The Business Model: Recent Developments and Future Research. *Journal of Management* 37 (4): 1019–1042.

6

Conclusion: The Future of eSports

Abstract The eSports industry is a highly complex environment that is continually evolving. Based on this innovativeness, there are ground-breaking changes that disrupt the industry every five years or so. Furthermore, many external stakeholders invest in eSports, creating a potential bubble, due to an overheated market. Such a development may result in a correction or a crisis, but it highlights the importance of creating a business model to monetize the audience. Besides the risk of not having a solid business model, eSports organizations need to govern the risk concerning future developments related to franchising, new markets, new games, and an ongoing fragmentation of the eSports industry. The eSports industry will, despite any events, grow, though the composition of stakeholders may change.

Keywords eSports • Franchise • Market growth • Fragmentation • Sustainability • Risk governance

© The Author(s) 2019
T. M. Scholz, *eSports is Business*, https://doi.org/10.1007/978-3-030-11199-1_6

Utilizing the Risks of eSports

It is undeniable that the eSports industry is growing exponentially at the moment and many new individuals and organizations are joining the eSports market. However, there is a clear risk of another bubble, primarily due to the amount of money flowing into eSports and existing eSports organizations. Although there is an ever-increasing market, and industry reports outbid each other regarding growth numbers, eSports is an emerging and volatile industry. Therefore, weak signals are perceptible that suggest a potential bubble, mimicking the situation concerning the Championship Gaming Series. But the good news is, if it happens, the eSports industry will bounce back and grow even higher. The question is, will it be a minor correction, a full-fledged crisis, or a potential crash of the eSports industry?

The underlying problem of eSports infused by outside money is a typical problem every organization is facing: how to create a business model that will lead to a steady stream of revenue. As the general manager of the eSports organization Immortals, Tomi 'lurppis' Kovanen, says: "No one in esports has found a way to monetize the fans" (Esmarch 2018). That statement is hyperbolical, but it fits the narrative of this book. At the moment, monetization of the audience is significantly low compared to traditional sports. A study by Berenberg states that in 2017 every sports fan could be translated into $54 revenue, while every eSports fan would bring only $1.8 revenue (Rosa 2018). These numbers may be rough estimates, but they highlight that it is necessary to have solid strategic management and to find a business model that allows the stakeholders to create a profitable and sustainable business model. In the current situation, many organizations are burning money in the hope that eSports will grow indefinitely and, because of that growth, the non-existing business model will magically create a profit that may lead to a return on investment.

Forbes (Ozanian et al. 2018) recently published a list of the biggest ~ in eSports and the value of these teams. Interestingly, this is a ~xample of numbers in eSports: they appear, and it is highly ~w those numbers were created. There is no argument that ~most prominent organization at the moment, but a value ~s disputable. Furthermore, the organization Echo Fox, being a newcomer and recently removing several squads (Cocke 2018), is valued at \$150 million, and Fnatic is valued at \$120 million. Echo Fox has no value creation or products besides being part of the franchise league of *LoL*. Fnatic, on the other hand, has its hardware line, a thriving merchandise business, one of the biggest brands in eSports, and is seen as an empire (Cuadrado 2017). The market is overheating, and the costs of creating a successful eSports organization will rise, but the majority of organizations are unable to translate the investment into something similar to a business model, a situation that may lead to another bubble bursting, despite the fact that the eSports industry is a place in which you can be innovative and reach an audience that many traditional organizations are desperate to achieve. Companies like DHL realized the potential of sponsorship of *Dota 2* tournaments from the ESL, but went beyond that by creating commercials that fit their products—for example, their EffiBOT acting as an in-game courier—and are true to the core of the scene (ESL 2018).

Besides the lack of strategic management, there is also a lack of discussion of the potential risks in eSports. Belief drives the general perception that eSports will grow and this may shroud the existing risks in eSports. In the short term, this may be the case; but in the long term, not everybody will survive this growth. Furthermore, eSports may increase, but the eSports environment will change, too. Concerning eSports titles especially, the industry is highly volatile. Games like *Overwatch* may become the next big eSports titles, or they could vanish in two years. There is an apparent risk in investing in the eSports industry, most importantly as nobody seems to be able to create and design a successful and long-running eSports title. This situation leads to two observations. Firstly, the strategic management needs to create business models that are dynamic, especially as markets may emerge abruptly. An exciting and upcoming field is the potential utilization of the sneakers professional players wear. Many players are equipped with a team-related outfit, but the sneakers are often the only way to show their individuality (Carpenter 2018). There is a business model in it, and the company K-Swiss has announced sneakers for the Immortals (Webster 2018). Secondly, if the business model is dynamic, the strategic management is flexible; as the market is highly volatile, risk management is not possible, but utilizing risks may be a way to steer the organization strategically. This concept is called risk governance (Stein and Wiedemann 2016), and it incorporates the complexity of the environment and "cannot take place in isolation. Nor is it something that can be applied in a standard way in all locations, political cultures, organizations and risk situations" (Renn 2008, p. 9). Risk governance sees risks from a strategic perspective and deals with the uncertainties (Hassler 2011) attached to risks and risk evaluations. Therefore, risk governance goes beyond risk management and the standard assessment of known threats.

Where the eSports industry is concerned, risk governance will become increasingly crucial to pursue in creating a sustainable business model. The eSports environment is constantly shifting due to the shift in the interests of the audience, a development that is observable in the context of upcoming eSports titles—for example, in the game *Rainbow Six*. This game may have slow growth, but it is becoming increasingly relevant for professional eSports organizations. Many big professional teams joined up with a *Rainbow Six* team early, and they have stuck with the game and the squad. The goal is to find new potential outlets for their business model proactively to have first-mover advantage. For many organizations, a successful way is to be part of a thriving game. Consequently, the risk governance of potential risks will be essential for the future of individual eSports stakeholders and for the eSports industry.

Based on the influx of money and many investors' fear of missing out, the eSports industry is currently overheating, and this will be a danger for the eSports industry. However, money is a systemic risk that could be resolved by undertaking professional strategic management and thinking about the business model. Any correction or crisis would only lead to the removal of unprofessional businesses. Three developments may have a groundbreaking influence on the understanding of eSports and how the eSports industry may evolve. Firstly, franchises are becoming increasingly popular and will have an impact on the way eSports titles interact with the eSports market. Secondly, frontiers will expand and new markets will be conquered. Finally, fragmentation of the industry will take place, as more stakeholders are involved in eSports than ever before. The eSports industry may become fragmented to a degree, and eSports should, ultimately, be used as a term describing all competitive gaming, similar to the utilization of sports. However, looking at the future of eSports, it is relevant to discuss those developments.

Franchise: A Gamble for Power

The franchise development is quite interesting, especially as it is a strategy from traditional sports to use in eSports and has failed before, as seen in the case of the Championship Gaming Series. Furthermore, the franchise strategy per se is not innovative or dynamic at all. There are the game developers and the few franchise owners, and that's it. This development is often sold as a way to stabilize growth and create a thriving environment for the eSports industry, but the assumption is that it is possible to have long, stable growth focused around one distinct game. It is striking to observe that this volatility in games and the connected innovation is seen as something terrible, as a system without structures and without governance—hence the Wild West. In every other industry, this volatility is appraised, and many organizations invest millions to infuse their organization with a start-up mentality. The eSports industry has a highly dynamic environment, combined with self-organization and self-governance, and can be seen as a liberal environment. The franchise idea is, in general, a move toward a static environment with top-down governance. It is crucial to highlight that static does not necessarily mean stable.

It is observable that the franchising strategies co-align with franchising models in North America. Franchising may lead to an increase in brand value and some form of consistency; the franchises in *Overwatch* and *League of Legends* may, eventually, lead to a specific brand consistency, but the initial signals are quite mixed. Looking at the rumors concerning the franchising for *LoL* in Europe, successful brands and long-time partners like the Unicorns of Love, Vodafone Giants, and H2K in cooperation with Paris Saint-Germain were rejected for the upcoming franchise (Byers 2018; Kolev 2018). In the North American league, various NBA teams bought a slot. However—and this is an apparent inconsistency—they refused to utilize their names: for example, the Houston Rockets team is called Clutch Gaming. In Europe, especially, it will be interesting to see which organizations will join the new league. However, removing the aspect of relegation will also remove some exciting stories for the audience.

However, there are several structural challenges for franchises in the future. With the current eSports evolution, many fans are not necessarily fans of a specific eSports organization, but rather supporters of a distinct player. The fans' allegiance will wander with the player, a phenomenon similar to that seen with Cristiano Ronaldo (Lewis 2018). The Overwatch League tries to counteract this development by paying a less competitive salary compared to other games and, furthermore, not allowing any competition to the Overwatch League. This development is highlighted in the following statement: "But it's hard to talk about 'Overwatch' without also talking about Overwatch League, a multi-hundred-million-dollar experiment that was carefully designed to look and feel like a traditional sports league to entice traditional sports conglomerates" (Partin 2018).

Although the franchise system is linked tightly with traditional sports, there are differences that may be harmful to the growth of franchises in eSports. First of all, there is a lack of a sustainable and reliable youth system in eSports. Without a collegiate system comparable to that seen in the NCAA, there is no potential youth structure for drafting talents and no way to create some form of balance. At the moment, the collegiate level seems to be an alternative route into eSports, but highly unregulated. Notably, in *Overwatch*, being a global league, it would mean that teams in other regions would require a similar structure to North America to create some form of balance. Furthermore, there is no salary cap in the franchises. The eSports organization can pay whatever it wants and get the people it wants. Franchising does not lead to an increase in consistency. Lacking a reliable draft system and a salary cap ultimately means that leagues following the franchise system have only a franchise lite system.

Another aspect of the current franchise trend is trying to create a local audience in relation to geolocation. There are several challenges with that. Firstly, it is difficult to develop a global league and have local events. Games in their respective cities will be stressful for the players: take a look at the Pacific Division in *Overwatch*, consisting of the Shanghai Dragons and the Dallas Fuel. Players would fly roughly a whole day to travel between these cities. Secondly, there is no real need for arenas in eSports, at least for the general league stages. The audience, at the moment, prefers arena events for big tournaments like the world finals after a whole season. Furthermore, it is important to highlight that the franchises in

North America are heavily subsidized in relation to arenas. The taxpayer partially subsidizes many arenas in the NFL and the NBA so the teams will stay in the city and attract businesses (Coates 2007; Kianka 2013). It is debatable whether this is a good investment on the part of the cities; however, these subsidies have helped many sports teams in North America to grow, and it is questionable if a similar development is possible in eSports in the near future.

Furthermore, there is an assumption that franchising will automatically lead to a potential increase in revenues, especially as revenues are shared between the game developers and the franchise owner. However, recent rumors hint that some franchises in *LoL* are up for sale, and recent layoffs strengthen this claim (Li 2018). The comment by former pro player William 'scarra' Li is particularly alarming: "They don't believe in the business model, and they want out" (Chouadria 2018). Although these may be rumors, the underlying message is clear: franchising does not lead to a sustainable business model, and any franchise owner has to find a way to monetize the audience. Many team owners still struggle to make a profit (Takahashi 2018).

The question that arises is whether eSports titles are even comparable to franchise leagues like the NBA. Andreas Thorstensson (2018), a long-time eSports veteran, raises the argument that eSports may be similar to circuit-based sports like golf and tennis. This analogy may be fitting for many games, and the success of *Counter-Strike* is testament to this comparison. Still, the franchise league may work for *Overwatch*, especially as it is tailored to be a franchise. However, it may not be the next big eSports title and will position itself in a niche. The future for *League of Legends* depends on its success in Europe and South Korea. China is already known to be tightly controlled and, in that case, a franchise makes no difference, while North America prefers the franchise system.

Frontier: Conquering New Markets

The eSports industry is still growing, and many markets are still underdeveloped; however, it is already observable that growth in specific regions may be stronger than in other areas. North America especially is lagging behind expectations. There is a noticeable growth, and many new eSports organizations have emerged in recent years, but there is an open discussion in the eSports industry as to whether it is possible to fill the arenas for big tournaments. The North American finals in *League of Legends* had some empty seats, the Intel Extreme Masters moved from Oakland to Chicago, and there are many other examples. It is true that the Overwatch League finals sold out the Barclay Arena in New York, but it was the first final of a popular eSports title. Outside North America, it seems surprisingly simple to fill arenas around the world. At the forefront of this enthusiastic audience is China.

At the same time, Europe may not be the innovative driver for the future of eSports. Although stakeholders like the ESL or Fnatic have a proven track record, they seem to have found a solid business model and are trying to improve their strategic management. This development is necessary for the potential upcoming crisis, but there are only a few new markets to conquer. There is space for monetization of the audience and to try to motivate female gamers to participate on the professional circuit. Furthermore, many European organizations can be seen as risk averse and therefore focusing on robust strategies to create a sustainable business model.

Although numbers in sports are often not reliable, and the numbers for eSports are even less reliable, according to ESC.watch (2018), in the recent world championship in *League of Legends*, the finals between Fnatic and Invictus Gaming attracted an audience of over 200 million viewers. Excluding the Chinese audience, the number drops to 2 million viewers. These numbers may be not entirely accurate, but it is certain that they outshine the global audience by far. Therefore, it is a logical development that the next International in *Dota 2* will be in Shanghai. Besides the massive market, Chinese corporations like Alibaba and Tencent have become essential to game developers. For example, Tencent owns Riot Games completely, has a majority in Supercell (*Clash of Clans*), owns 40% of Epic Games (*Fortnite*), has a minority stake in Activision Blizzard, and has other investments in many different companies. Tencent especially seems to be becoming a strong force in eSports, and it may even be the case that it will become the dominating force in the eSports industry in this "golden period" (Tencent 2018), despite recent governmental regulations that led to a loss in value of $20 billion (Roantree and Glenn 2018). The franchise development by Riot Games seemed to be rooted in the demand for Tencent to grow more profitable (Rodriguez 2018). Nevertheless, China will be the dominant force in the coming years of eSports (Russell 2018), and the eSports market in China could potentially grow to $1.5 billion in 2020 (Valentine 2018).

Besides China, the next markets to conquer will be Japan and countries in Southeast Asia. In Japan especially, it will be interesting to see the development, as it is one of the homelands of video games. Japan gave the world Nintendo, Sony, and a vast number of interesting video games. It has the people and the infrastructure, but still there is no thriving eSports industry. That may change in the coming years, as seen with the *Clash Royale* world finals held in Tokyo: "Japan … could be on the rise as an esports hub" (Murray 2018). The eSports organization that can enter Japan successfully will conquer a market that seems perfect for eSports. The same is true for any other country in Southeast Asia, and several tournaments have revealed the potential. These countries also have an excellent infrastructure and a young demographic. Such countries will start to shape the eSports industry in the near future and maybe revitalize South Korea as well. South Korea seems at the moment to be saturated and to have hit a ceiling and has consequently become inert in recent years. However, this country has an existing eSports infrastructure as well as many highly trained talents. South Korea could become a developer for the growth of eSports in Asia, and this strategy may help foster growth in South Korea.

The global south will require more time, as the infrastructure is still not as reliable as in the global north. However, with the current move toward eSports titles on mobiles, this may change faster than is thought. It is becoming evident that eSports have space to grow, but, as for any internationalization strategy, it is essential to understand the regional market. Especially in eSports, regional differences are observable in relation to the games that are played. Adapting to the cultural specifics will be necessary to enter those regional markets.

Fragmentation: Division of the eSports Industry

Finally, a recent development may change the understanding of eSports fundamentally. It seems that the eSports industry is not a winner-takes-all market, as seen in many other emerging technology markets, but rather an industry in which the market is shared among a variety of eSports titles and eSports organizations. Especially concerning eSports titles, after an initial explosion, growth eases, and games like *Dota 2* reveal a stable viewership. Even for the new kid on the block, *Fortnite*, the numbers seem to grow slowly. The numbers for any eSports title and the connected business model network may have a distinct ceiling that the game can reach but not go beyond. This development may highlight a limit to diffusion as well as a degree of potential saturation. Although this observation may be overshadowed by the idea that there are still markets to conquer, in general, there seems to be a certain limit to the audience that can be bound to a game. The eSports industry may grow, but the games have a distinct market saturation. This development will also mean that more eSports titles can participate in the eSports industry, leading to an increase in fragmentation.

Furthermore, an increase in eSports titles will lead to a reduction of the power of the game developer, as well as motivating other game developers to create eSports titles. The recent hype around Battle Royale led to various games with an eSports tournament landscape, most predominantly *Fortnite* and *PUBG*. Both game developers, in cooperation with tournament organizers and the community, are trying to find the right way to create a tournament landscape for their game. At the same time, existing games like *League of Legends* and *Counter-Strike* strive to enhance their longevity. Also, many other stakeholders are joining the eSports industry, adding to the fragmentation. In general, the eSports industry will become more diverse, increasing the competition and highlighting the importance of a sustainable business model within the business model network of eSports. The eSports industry may grow more fragmented, but the general principles of coopetition, co-destiny, and convergence will be increasingly important for the growth of the business model. With this crisis looming, the focus will be on the business model, and that is a valuable lesson to learn. Surviving in the eSports industry is based on strategic management and the realization that creating a business will require the support of the various stakeholders in the eSports industry. In the future, there may be a fragmentation that may only lead to a business model network for a distinct eSports title, but it may also necessitate a meta-business model network for the eSports industry as a whole.

References

Byers, Preston. 2018. Splyce, H2K, and Paris Saint-Germain Have Reportedly Been Declined EU LCS Franchising Spots. Accessed 2 November 2018. https://dotesports.com/league-of-legends/news/splyce-h2k-and-paris-saint-germain-have-reportedly-been-declined-eu-lcs-franchising-spots.

Carpenter, Nicole. 2018. Esports Sneakerheads: How OWL is Bringing Street Style to Pro Gaming. Accessed 2 November 2018. https://dotesports.com/overwatch/news/ow-league-fashion-nyxl-gesture-london-spitfire-31672.

Chouadria, Adel. 2018. Scarra Says Despite LCS Franchising, North American LCS Teams are Up for Sale. Accessed 2 November 2018. https://cybersport.com/post/some-north-american-lcs-teams-reportedly-up-sale.

Coates, Dennis. 2007. Stadiums and Arenas: Economic Development or Economic Redistribution? *Contemporary Economic Policy* 25 (4): 565–577.

Cocke, Taylor. 2018. Cuts at Infinite Esports and Echo Fox Signal an Esports Correction, Not Trouble. Accessed 2 November 2018. https://esportsob-server.com/infinite-esports-echo-fox-cuts.

Cuadrado, Patrick S. 2017. How a Gaming 'Fnatic' Built an eSports Empire. Accessed 2 November 2018. https://edition.cnn.com/2016/06/02/sport/esports-fnatic-team-profile-olofmeister.

ESC.watch. 2018. 2018 World Championship. Accessed 2 November 2018. https://esc.watch/tournaments/lol/worlds-2018.

ESL. 2018. Code King: DHL Courier EffiBot Delivers Salves. Accessed 2 November 2018. https://youtu.be/JRHYpil7b6M.

Esmarch, Lars. 2018. Immortals GM Lurppis: 'No One in Esports Has Found a Way to Monetize the Fans'. Accessed 2 November 2018. https://www.hltv.org/news/24001/immortals-gm-lurppis-no-one-in-esports-has-found-a-way-to-monetize-the-fans.

Hassler, Björn. 2011. Accidental Versus Operational Oil Spills from Shipping in the Baltic Sea: Risk Governance and Management Strategies. *Ambio* 40 (2): 170–178.

Kianka, Tim. 2013. Subsidizing Billionaires: How Your Money is Being Used to Construct Professional Sports Stadiums. Accessed 2 November 2018. http://lawweb2009.law.villanova.edu/sportslaw/?p=1853.

Kolev, Radoslav. 2018. Giants, ROCCAT and Unicorns of Love Reportedly Denied EU LCS Franchise Spot. Accessed 2 November 2018. https://cyber-sport.com/post/giants-roccat-uol-denied-eu-lcs-franchise.

Lewis, Aimee. 2018. Has the Digital Age Changed Football Fans. Accessed 2 November 2018. https://edition.cnn.com/2018/08/17/football/cristiano-ronaldo-juventus-social-media-fans-china-spt-intl/index.html.

Li, Xing. 2018. League Personality William 'Scarra' Li Hints at Financial Problems in the NA LCS. Accessed 2 November 2018. https://dotesports.com/league-of-legends/news/league-personality-william-scarra-li-hints-at-financial-problems-in-the-na-lcs.

Murray, Trent. 2018. Clash Royale League World Finals to be Held in Tokyo. Accessed 2 November 2018. https://esportsobserver.com/clash-royale-league-finals-tokyo.

Ozanian, Mike, Christina Settimi, and Matt Perez. 2018. The World's Most Valuable Esports Companies. Accessed 2 November 2018. https://www.forbes.com/sites/mikeozanian/2018/10/23/the-worlds-most-valuable-esports-companies-1/#1d3194396a6e.

Partin, Will. 2018. Blizzard's Ban on Third-Party Overwatch Apps was Never About Competitive Integrity. Accessed 2 November 2018. https://variety.com/2018/gaming/columns/blizzards-ban-on-third-party-overwatch-apps-was-never-about-competitive-integrity-1202961745.

Renn, Ortwin. 2008. *Risk Governance: Coping with Uncertainty in a Complex World*. London: Earthscan.

Roantree, Anne Marie and Elias Glenn. 2018. Tencent Loses $20 Billion in Value After China Attacks Myopia with Gaming Curbs. Accessed 2 November 2018. https://www.reuters.com/article/us-china-gaming/tencent-loses-20-billion-in-value-after-china-attacks-myopia-with-gaming-curbs-idUSKCN1LF25B.

Rodriguez, Veronika. 2018. Relationship Between Riot Games and Tencent is Reportedly Deteriorating. Accessed 2 November 2018. https://www.dbltap.com/posts/6143284-relationship-between-riot-games-and-tencent-is-reportedly-deteriorating.

Rosa, Jeremy. 2018. Esports: What Is It and Is It Real. Accessed 2 November 2018. http://blogs.ci.com/harbour/jeremy-rosa/esports-what-it-and-it-real.

Russell, Chris. 2018. China Stands Ready to Lead eSports Globally. Accessed 2 November 2018. http://knowledge.ckgsb.edu.cn/2017/09/18/technology/esports-in-china-lead-globally.

Stein, Volker, and Arnd Wiedemann. 2016. Risk Governance: Conceptualization, Tasks, and Research Agenda. *Journal of Business Economics* 86 (8): 813–836.

Takahashi, Dean. 2018. Overwatch League Commissioner Nate Nanzer: Esports Profits are Light at the End of the Tunnel. Accessed 2 November 2018. https://venturebeat.com/2018/09/29/overwatch-league-commissioner-nate-nanzer-esports-profits-are-light-at-the-end-of-the-tunnel.

Tencent. 2018. Cheng Wu: Tencent Esports Will Realize New Power in the In-Depth Layout Year of Esports Industry. Accessed 2 November 2018. http://www.prnewswire.co.uk/news-releases/cheng-wu-tencent-esports-will-realize-new-power-in-the-in-depth-layout-year-of-esports-industry-685907382.html.

Thorstensson, Andreas. 2018. Tweet. Accessed 2 November 2018. https://twitter.com/andreas/status/1055005556258287622.

Valentine, Rebekah. 2018. Tencent: Chinese Esports Market Expected to Grow to $1.5 Billion in 2020. Accessed 2 November 2018. https://www.gamesindustry.biz/articles/2018-06-27-tencent-chinese-esports-market-expected-to-grow-to-usd1-5-billion-in-2020.

Webster, Andrew. 2018. K-Swiss is Designing a Pair of Sneakers for an E-sports Team. Accessed 2 November 2018. https://www.theverge.com/2018/4/27/17290280/k-swiss-esports-sneakers-immortals.

Index

© The Author(s) 2019
T. M. Scholz, *eSports is Business*, https://doi.org/10.1007/978-3-030-11199-1

CPSIA information can be obtained
at www.ICGtesting.com
Printed in the USA
LVHW081819221220
674905LV00010B/513